From BORSCH to BURGERS

A Cross-Cultural Memoir

Ruslana A. Westerlund

*To Renata
From Ruslana
Ukraine will
prevail!
6.7.22*

Cover design by Dmytro Komar
Edited by Carolyn Schott
Layout design by Deborah Stocco

Ruslana Westerlund
Visit my website at www.ruslanawesterlund.com

Printed in the United States of America

First Printing: August 2019
Arkangel Creations

ISBN: 978-1-0795-6664-2

Table of Contents

Table of Contents

Dedication

I dedicate this book to my mom first and foremost. Mom, you gave me life. And then you let go of me and let me be on my own, away from the potatoes and the back-breaking "vegetable gardens." You made it possible for me to come to "America" (as you always called the United States) by asking Caryl Bloem to take me with her. Thank you, Mom. I'm sorry you are not able to read my book. I'll tell you about it when we see each other again.

My Mom and Dad. Summer 2017.

Dad, hang in there. You have always been my inspiration. I love you. Thank you for bringing me in your old Zaporozhets to Cherkassy to study English. It has opened so many doors for me, but I realize it also contributed to our family living an ocean and a continent apart.

Thank you, Caryl, for your generosity and for being willing to take a risk by welcoming a stranger to live in your home for three years! Thank you for not questioning whether the practice of bribes, a standard practice in our corrupt society, was right, but for helping me through the visa process. Thank you for persevering through the invitation process and for trusting in God, despite the circumstances.

Ron, thank you for years of patience, particularly for these new big things: teaching me how to water ski and how to deal with ears full of water and sore muscles the day after; taking me on road trips from Boston to San Diego and up to Yellowstone; and teaching me how to drive at the age of 22! I will never forget the 10 national parks in 10 days and 5,000 miles of road trippin'! Thank you for not killing me when I almost caused an accident when learning how to drive. I'm sorry if this brings up traumatic memories that you buried deep down, hoping they would never re-surface. I also learned from you how to avoid speeding tickets. I've only gotten one in Wisconsin (so far).

Honey Rob, thank you for believing in me before I believed in myself. It was true with my doctorate and it's also true with this book. Thank you for saying these words, "Ru, you should write a memoir." Thank you for not quitting when editing this book. Thank you for your gentle ways of correcting my overuse of the article *the* and for my idiosyncratic overlay of Ukrainian on English. Thank you for persisting in trying to reach my diverse audiences through my stories told here.

My boys Julian and Nicky, thanks for teaching me about American pop culture and superheroes. I still confuse Marvel and DC, but I know 100% that Superman can't survive without kryptonite (or is it the other way around?) and Ironman has a robot exoskeleton. One is DC and the other one is Marvel, but don't ask me which is which. You also taught me a lot about the English language, especially the language of your teen cliques and online communities. I'm not sure what "ulting" means, so I consulted an online dictionary but the word hasn't been added yet. You guys are developing your language so fast, the dictionary "committee" can't keep up.

Also, to everyone who asked me questions such as "So how do you celebrate Thanksgiving in Ukraine?", "What do you do for the 4th of July?" (just kidding, I didn't get that one yet), "Where are you from, from?", "What do you mean you don't do small talk in Ukraine?", "How did you two meet?", "Are your children bilingual?", "What was it like to survive communism?", and "How do you pronounce your name again?" I answer all these questions and more in this book.

I also dedicate this book to every single person who has contributed to my cross-cultural awareness and all of you who have enriched my life in ways I couldn't have done by myself. You have stretched me and challenged me; you have contributed to my ever-growing understanding of what it means to live cross-culturally. I strive to make those encounters mutually enriching. You know who you are.

Thank you.

Note from the Author

If I had it my way, I would have titled this book *From Monocle to Kaleidoscope: Viewing the World Through Cultural Bi-focals—A Mirror and Window to the World of Transcendent Belonging.* Fortunately, I was advised *against* using these titles and stuck with *From Borsch to Burgers* (The spelling of borsch is explained in chapter 10). And yet, this is a memoir of a cross-cultural journey, a remembrance of times past, which are still alive and current within my heart, soul, and mind. Cross-cultural remembering is as much about recalling immutable memories as it is about documenting the dynamic and iterative process of becoming, the journey of the self through new terrains. For many immigrants, their journey to the undiscovered country of their future cultural identity takes them through more than just new lands, but also through terrains of culture, language, and worldview. A common stage for the traveler is when the understanding of their new identity is bogged down in a La Brea tar pit of self-perception, places where we muck through trying to understand our unresolved cultural identity. Most immigrants, knowingly or unknowingly, wrestle with the question of cultural identity as soon as their culture shock wears off and the excitement about their new location, architecture, sights and sounds cools down (as identified by Eva Hoffman in her memoir *Lost in Translation: My Life in a New Language*). In that process, we realize that we are no longer just our original ethnic selves, contained in clearly outlined cultural and linguistic boxes, but we are in the process of becoming something new. Our boxes expand and metamorphose into something new.

Memoirs are also about capturing our memories before they escape. Many of us live in the "here and now, you and me" and we don't think to pause to realize that we are losing life's precious moments, just like the morning dew evaporates instantly as soon as the sun hits the grass. Our feet hit the ground at the sound of the alarm and we rush through our lives without realizing how fast we gain and how quickly we lose our memories. I used to live my life in a hurry until my mom passed away. It wasn't until she was gone that I stopped to think about how her life stories had left with her. There are no written records left behind documenting her life. I don't even have her voice recorded. When my grandma Baba Manya passed away, a generation of stories was buried with her, but they don't have to stay there. They can be unearthed and restored through my writing, through my remembering. When I die one day, I'll have my stories recorded here.

One person told me that I am too young to write a memoir, but I disagreed because I already have forgotten so much. Especially the cross-cultural experiences: how long was my culture shock? When did my identities start expanding? When did I decide that I'm no longer just Ukrainian, but Ukrainian-American? What were the feelings that accompanied each stage? What were the stages? What were my questions about this process? What were my fears? What were my losses? What were my gains?

To capture my cross-cultural rememberings in ink facilitates the cathartic process of understanding my longing. A pilgrim who travels to a new land has a longing to belong without compromising her true self at the same time. She fears to lose herself while adjusting to her new culture. Also, anyone who leaves their home longs for a place, as in the word *hiraeth*, a Welsh concept of longing for home, for a place you cannot return to. For me, *hiraeth* means both: longing for a place where I belong and longing for a home.

Whenever I visit Ukraine, I feel like I'm a visitor. I don't fit in there any-more— culturally or otherwise. Not even in my own home where I grew up. The house feels different. The ceilings are lower. The river is narrower. The скосогори (*skosohori)* berms on each side of the potato field are not as steep as they were when I was a child. This happens to everybody who grows up. It's not a unique immigrant phenomenon by any means. I long to feel at home in my home, but it's not possible anymore, because I am not the same person. In the words of Nelson Mandela, "There is nothing like returning to a place that remains unchanged to find the ways in which you yourself have altered."

But in other ways, everything has changed: children grew up, neighbors have passed away, and new babies have been born. Everything has changed, absolutely everything, except for the condition of the road that leads me home. It still remains unpaved and somehow it gives me a feeling of comfort to know that there is a piece of my childhood that has stayed the same.

I was born in 1973 and left Ukraine in 1995. I am writing about the years in between. Things have changed rapidly since 1995. I ask that you read my descriptions as artifacts of those years. In some accounts, I tried to speak to more recent changes because I am still connected to the place where *моя пуповина захована* (my umbilical cord is buried). But I've learned that keeping up to date with the rapid changes in Ukraine has been more challenging and, on many occasions, emotionally draining. I apologize for inaccuracies or not being up to date on current trends. If some descriptions are antiquated, that's on purpose because they represent the Ukraine that I knew back then.

In this memoir I write about rural Ukraine, the land I know best and is dearest to me. Urban Ukraine is light years ahead of the countryside, where the infrastructure is more developed, the cultural life is richer with museums, galleries, and coffee shops, and grocery stores are more abundant. It is in stark contrast to the dirt roads and one-room-size "grocery" stores in the forgotten villages because the money never leaves Kyiv, getting pocketed by greedy politicians. It's like describing life in the village of Cross Plains,

Wisconsin, and using it as an example of what all of America is like. To my readers who don't know Ukraine, be careful not to conceptualize all of Ukraine as a whole based on an account of Ukraine with a limited scope of time and place. Take this account as *my* version of *my* slice of Ukraine, *my* perceptions of Ukraine at a particular time and place.

I am also writing to my future self: Remember that your perceptions will grow as you age and your "enlightenment" will also change. So, forgive yourself in the future for the accounts described here and cherish them as artifacts of your introspection at this point in time.

Borrowing from Eva Hoffman: We make sense of the world through our own lens; we sift the new culture through the sieve of our own culture. So, I ask forgiveness for painting your culture with my own brush. That's the only way that we are able to understand the new.

Prologue

It is the summer of 2008, the year the movie WALL-E is released. My boys, Julian and Nicky, are 6 and 3. We are huddled in our basement in front of the TV, snuggling together under the blankets. I watch this movie through the eyes of a mother and an immigrant, comparing the moving images I see on the screen with the still memories of my own life. This PIXAR production depicts the adventures of a good-hearted robot who is rocketed onto a journey where he encounters a culture unlike his own. I watch it and see parallels between WALL-E's adventure and my own. WALL-E passes his days alone on Earth, collecting trinkets and treasures from amongst the heaps of garbage covering the planet.

There is a scene in which WALL-E holds up a spork and can't figure out which collection of utensils to add it to: is it a fork or is it a spoon? It's neither and it's both. As a bicultural person who was raised in Ukraine but lived most of her adult life in the U.S., I feel like a spork most of the time: a little bit Ukrainian, a little bit American, and a whole lot of "in between." I've lived in the U.S. since 1995, but most Americans still view me as a foreigner, which is a natural thing to do because I'm literally not from here. It happens when people ask me questions about where my name is from or what the origin of my accent is. When I order my coffee at a local coffee shop and just want to get on with my day, I get "Where are you from?" I want to say I'm from Minnesota, but they don't mean that. They mean where are you from, from? When I say, "I'm from Ukraine," they ask, "Do you know so and so from the Ural Mountains?" or "It must be so cold because it's close to Siberia." I want to say, and sometimes I do when I'm in a feisty mood, "Well, Siberia is actually closer to the U.S. than Ukraine."

They assume Ukraine is part of Russia, something Ukrainians have been fighting against since Moscow appeared out of a swamp in the 13th century.

When I return to visit my family in Ukraine, I don't always feel like I fit in there either. In some aspects, I feel like I am a foreigner in my own land. I forget my own language, and when I speak, it comes out as if translated from English. My nephew Igor says, "Ru, your Ukrainian is high intermediate." While this may make me feel as if I'm stuck between two cultures, neither fully American and not fully Ukrainian anymore, I celebrate the advantage of being able to embrace both cultures and to be truly global.

We don't hold a spork and say, "this is designed so poorly." No, we find it innovative, useful, flexible, adaptable, and an example of out-of-the-box thinking. It belongs with the forks *and* the spoons, and yet it is in a class of its own. After decades in a new culture, I've become a new me: a spoon and fork combination. I don't have to be only one or the other—either Ukrainian or American. I can be both. I can be a hyphenated American, just like most immigrants are. So, this story is about becoming a spork, and figuring out how to fit in and how to remain unique.

This book could not have been written back when I first arrived in the U.S. back in 1995. One has to live on both sides of the cross-cultural border long enough to be able to analyze the cultural differences, to appreciate values found on both sides, and to be able to develop a sense of humor when experiencing cultural clashes. I wouldn't have been able to write this book if I were processing these cross-cultural differences by myself because most people, who haven't experienced more than their own hometown or have never left it literally and figuratively, aren't able to conceive of more than one worldview. I spent many years observing the cultural differences between the Ukrainian and American people, but at first, I was only able to process what I learned from a Ukrainian worldview. It's not until I juxtapose my worldview against another that the differences are clarified.

As I began to conceptualize this book, I realized that I needed another thinker to think with: my husband "honey Rob." Rob is a thinker with a capital T. If you think deep conceptual thoughts (more than "What are we having for dinner?"), you are a thinker with a capital T. Rob thinks big abstract thoughts all the time, even when we are having dinner. When I enter his thought space, interjecting new thoughts and ideas, his brain goes into "Recalculating ... Recalculating" mode (like a GPS getting new instructions). When my worldview enters Rob's worldview, it's like two worlds colliding. This book is richer because of those two worlds colliding when we met on October 31, 1997.

I entertained the idea of chronicling my cross-cultural journey for a while, but I wasn't ready yet, and I didn't know why. I'd had plenty of experiences, but not enough "meta" in the meta-analysis. In the same way an artist must establish an aesthetic distance from her subject, a memoirist must establish a temporal distance from her experiences to gain a proper perspective. One can't analyze anything when being stuck in a constant state of confusion or being defensive or judgmental. One clear vision I had for this book from the beginning was to write about the serious business of cross-cultural living in a humorous way. Humor is hard to write, especially about cross-cultural matters and when there is something only I, and not anyone else, finds humorous. But as I continued writing, the humor fizzled out, and it couldn't be forced, so it's sprinkled throughout. You'll be lucky if you find it. I realized halfway through the book that I couldn't pull off a Frank McCourt and his artful skills of creating a tragicomedy: a comedy out of a tragedy. Although my cross-cultural sense-making wasn't tragical, some moments of learning English were borderline disastrous. But the point of sharing my language-learning challenges in the United States is not to elicit pity but to build awareness, in a humorous way, of how our language works and the spoken and unspoken rules about the culture I observed.

I intend for the stories here to entertain and enlighten, reflect and think. I hope that this book is both a window and a mirror. It functions as a mirror in a way for me to reflect on my own story, my culture, and my cross-cultural journey. And it serves as a window for my readers to learn from my story and catch a glimpse into one immigrant's journey. We cannot truly know ourselves until we learn about others. Because of getting to know so many of you, I've learned more about myself. Hopefully, it does the same for you. My cross-cultural living has enriched my life in many ways. I'm thankful to every one of you who have been part of this journey.

This book is as much about me learning a new culture as it is about me teaching others about my own. Cross-cultural exchange should be like a two-way street. For example, "You are in the world's greatest country, 'Merica. Learn our ways. Eat our food. Speak our language." My approach is more like: "Yes, teach me your ways and also, would you like to learn about Ukrainian food? Would you like to learn how to speak my language? Would you like to understand why I say things the way I do?"

Describing my cross-cultural insights and my life in post-Soviet Ukraine will hopefully provide my readers with an opportunity to expand and enrich their understanding of self and others so they can truly learn how to understand that which is different from themselves. As I reflected on my original invitation to the U.S., one of the purposes of my visit was to "promote understanding between our nations and promote world peace." I hope that the work I've done in education, ministry, and my daily encounters with you, has indeed contributed to a cross-cultural understanding. I have tried to document my own journey of understanding the new culture better. By no means is that journey complete. I hope you enjoy reading about it as much as I enjoyed writing it. Living it, though, wasn't always easy. Thank you for coming alongside me in this process.

~ Ruslana

CHAPTER 1

"What Was It Like Growing Up in Ukraine?"

My *Raison D'être* in Buzhanka

It's the summer of 2018, the year my mom passed away. My brother's family and I are helping my dad harvest potatoes. We are slaving away in the field, sweating under the hot August sun. But we are happy to be together. The work seems lighter.

"*Bodik, подай відро на малу картоплю* (Hand me that bucket for the small-size potatoes)," I tell my brother.

"*Тут велика картопля* (The big potatoes go in this bucket)," he says, pointing at an old black plastic bucket. This is how we sort potatoes.

Potatoes don't grow pre-sorted by size like they are found in a grocery store. Ukrainian farmers separate them by three sizes: large ones for eating; medium for planting the next year; and small, bruised, and damaged ones for the pigs. But this is 2018 and we are grown adults; this time we are joined by the third generation of potato workers, our children, picking potatoes in the same field where we spent our entire childhood.

"*Ри, завдай мішок,* (lift the sack up on my back)," Dad calls. I lift the 100-pound sack onto my dad's back and he carries it to the cellar. These are typical conversations your average village Ukrainians who are still able to walk and work have as they harvest potatoes. Through these actions

19

and conversations in 2018, I get flashbacks to my childhood from 1980 to 1990.

I don't know if you ever pondered your purpose for being born into this world when you were young, but as for me, I figure out in fourth grade that I am born into this world to sort, plant, weed, hoe, *nідгортаmи* (*pidhortahti*), weed again, cull bugs from the leaves, dig, sort, dice, fry, stew, boil, and eat potatoes. The word *pidhortahti*

A day in the life of a typical Ukrainian farming family, from left to right: my brother, his wife Natasha, their kids Artem and Diana, and my dad Anatoliy.

doesn't have an equivalent in English because the concept doesn't exist. It means to use a hoe to scoop up soil and make rounded mounds of dirt around a potato plant. This process of cultivating a potato field might sound culturally romantic and quaint, reminiscent of photos from a 1950s National Geographic depicting happy laborers in a potato field on a collective farm in the Soviet Union, but let me clear up this misconception. Laboring in a potato field all day is pure hell if you ask me. It's not like a therapy garden in your backyard where you can go out and trim daisies for an hour to blow off some steam. It's at least two acres and months of back-breaking, sweaty, and callus-inducing work.

The reason that word doesn't exist in English is that potato planting in modern-day industrialized nations (post-1900) is mechanized. Mechanized is the word we use when people use a tractor and don't have to make one hundred thousand individual holes with their spade. And I do mean spade, not a shovel. In Ukraine, we know the difference between the two, because a shovel is for shoveling pig manure, and a spade is for digging in the soil, and you don't want to confuse the two. Because harvesting was not done by a tractor when I was young (only recently did Dad fabricate his own equipment to do that), we have to locate each mound of dirt and dig up the potatoes with a spade. And you had to do that for the entire two-acre field.

I can't imagine a summer without potatoes. In my 10-year-old head, I don't know what that would look like because my whole existence is defined by potatoes. I believe with every fiber of my being that Ukrainians have always grown potatoes, but I recently discovered that this is not true and that potatoes become a thing of the 20th century. In the 18th and 19th centuries, the crop didn't do so well and it took 200 years for the crop to adapt to the Ukrainian climate. Two hundred years ago, Ukrainians grew potatoes in small quantities for starch and alcohol.

With this knowledge of how recent the development of the Ukrainian potato crop is, all of a sudden I have a glimmer of hope that maybe there is life without potatoes, after all. But then, what would Ukrainians do with themselves? I wonder about what they will use to fill their *vareniki* (pierogies) with in a world without potatoes! I wonder about all the children who grew up before the potato, in the 18th and 19th centuries. I see them bored out of their minds, roaming freely on the steppes before those steppes were bulldozed and turned into potato fields. I can hear the children calling out to one another, saying, "Vasya, let's just roll in the grass and feel the blades with our bare feet as we run through the fields. Come and catch me, if you can!" They don't know the pain in their lower backs from working the potatoes, and the only sunburn they get is from bathing in the sun, running through the steppes and not from being bent over with their backs to the sun.

According to the Farm and Agricultural Organization of the United Nations, "around half of the country's 1.5 million hectares of potato farms are located on the black soils [*chernozem*] of the forest-steppe zone in central Ukraine, although the best yields are obtained in the Polissya wetlands of the north." Just Google the map. Buzhanka is smack dab in the middle of central Ukraine. It's as central as it gets! I now realize that I grew up in the potato growing capital of Ukraine where my destiny was pre-determined by the chernozem of the former forest-steppe Ukraine when the Scythians roamed the free land.

It takes about a week for weeds to grow back after weeding, so in the interim, we engage in a hunt and destroy mission of Colorado beetles. There are rumors that the "evil Americans" conspired against us, executing a plot against our country, using Colorado beetles as a biological agent. I grow up believing this is true. It has to be because it is published in the Soviet paper called *ПРАВДА* (*Pravda*), which means the "Communist Truth," so we know every word is good as pure gold. If you don't believe the Communist Truth, you end up in the gulags. The gulags were a system of forced labor camps established during Stalin's reign as dictator of the Soviet Union. The gulags were different from the summer Pioneer camps where we children sing happy songs about Lenin and the glorious Party, do calisthenics in the morning, and dance around a campfire at night. Yes, in the gulags you do live in cabins, but they work you to death, just for being a Baptist, a non-conformist, part of the intelligentsia, or composing classical music that sounds too Western. So even today, I am still wondering if my Communist Truth newspaper told me the truth about the Colorado beetles. I'm not even sure that Colorado beetles are from Colorado. Now to all my friends in Colorado who are reading this book, I have a question for you: Do you have a bug that has stripes on its back and is fat and juicy when you step on it with guts oozing out its sides, and it eats potatoes for breakfast, second breakfast, elevenses, lunch, dinner, and snack time? If you do, let me know. Maybe *Pravda* was telling the truth after all.

Hiding the Weeds and Living Footloose & Cancer-free

"*Люда, пішли на пляж!* (Luda, let's go to the beach!)" I call out to my best friend. She responds, "We have to *sapati* and weed potatoes. Let's do my field first and then we'll go over to work your fields."

I am 11 years old and it's a hot summer day. I, along with many other young children, are given responsibilities to hoe (*sapati*), weed, and *pidhortati* potatoes. Imagine having to spend your summer vacation bent over ten thousand potato mounds, *pidhortating* under the blazing sun, pulling weeds and killing bugs? Let me tell you, it is no vacation. After all day in the field, my sister and I walk home bent over like our Ukrainian folktale villain, an old witch named Baba Yaga. If you haven't done that kind of work for hours on end, you have no idea how bad it is. There are no child labor rules in the Soviet Union. In fact, child labor is the rule. You know the saying, "Whatever doesn't kill you, makes you stronger?" Well, that's now my life motto. This is where my work ethic comes from. As a child, if I have lower back pain, or get a paper cut, or stub a toe, my mom tells me "*заживе, як на собаці*" ("it will heal as fast as on a dog"). Mom gives me a *podorozhnik* (plantain) leaf to apply to the wound. She teaches me how to spit on it first to clean off the dust and then apply to the scrapes and bruises. It stops the bleeding and serves as an antiseptic.

In the U.S., the plantain grows everywhere but no one uses it for medicinal purposes the way my mom did. Here, most mothers of young children carry a box of Band-Aids and a tube of Neosporin. I am taught that the American way is always the right way because you don't want germs from your spit to go into an open wound or scrape. I never will teach my boys how to stop bleeding with a plantain leaf. Another piece of wisdom about the benefits of herbal medicine dies with me.

When I come to the U.S., I see french fries served as fast food and I have flashbacks to my potato fields and our summer kitchen. Our summer kitchen is a place where we cook and eat in the summer to avoid overheating the house. My mom, my sister, and I work there daily julienning potatoes and frying them in lard as a fast food supper. That's how we make our fast food. There are no hash browns or tater tots that come in a bag preserved with chemicals "for freshness" (can you see an oxymoron there?). There's no McDonald's with a drive-through because our wonderful government in the 1980s doesn't allow McDonald's and other Western influences to pollute the minds and poison the bodies of our children. Thanks to my Soviet government, I never grew up with processed foods or junk food that comes with a toy in a bag. Glory to the Communist Party for that, right? We grew up with homemade fries, cooked in lard and bits of *salo* (Ukrainian unprocessed, uncured bacon).

It's in the middle of July, and the river is calling us to swim. The beach is so inviting, beckoning us to come to sunbathe, talk with our friends, and eat sunflower seeds, but the potato fields are also calling us for more weeding and hoeing. My best friend Luda and I often pair up for potato weeding, doing her field first and then mine. By the time we get to mine, we are just exhausted. We want to go swimming. We are kids. We are tired kids. We are tired, exhausted 11-year-old kids who just want a break from this potato purgatory. By the way, I hope there are no potatoes in heaven, and if there are, I hope they grow themselves. I'll be growing lavender instead. It looks and smells better than potatoes, and the Colorado beetles won't eat the leaves off it.

Being the hard-working but exhausted kids that we are, we come up with a brilliant idea. Instead of pulling the weeds, we think it would be a really good idea to cover them up by making bigger dirt mounds. We do that really fast and think of ourselves as being very efficient, plus we envision that the dirt mounds will be nice and fat, making it so much easier to find them later when harvesting. As soon as we are done, we throw our hoes on the ground and run to the river to swim.

My mom gets home from work … she praises us for our efficiency, but the words of praise she spews forth sound suspiciously like yelling and accusations of laziness. She isn't a happy camper, as you guys say it in English. We are also pretty disappointed to discover that the stubborn weeds force their way through the dirt and are visible the next day.

Thirty years later, telling this story is now bitter-sweet. Luda is fighting for her life against cancer as I write these words. It has

My friend Luda and I under the canopy of grapes at her house, Summer 2018.

spread into her lymph nodes, and chemo is killing her kidneys. Last summer when I went to Ukraine, we reminisced about this same story—potato fields, the river, and my mom yelling. My mom passed away last summer, also from cancer. So I'm sharing this story in this chapter not only because potatoes are important to talk about, but also because this story gives me one more chance to relive my childhood and remember my mom, young and full of life as she yells at the top of her lungs and we giggle, hiding from her wrath. As I write these words, tears roll down my cheeks because the story is allowing me to be in the past for one more moment when my mom is alive, Luda and I are 11, and there is no cancer.

"Potatoes are Second Bread"

It's 2018. I am in Ukraine for my nephew's wedding. My brother and his family and I are home in Buzhanka, helping my dad after our mom passed away earlier this year. My brother and I sit down to talk to dad after harvesting 1,200 pounds of potatoes, enough to feed him and the pigs for a year. My brother asks my dad, "How much can you sell these potatoes for?" He replies, "About 1,800 hryvna?" My brother calculates into euros and I do a quick exchange in my head to American dollars and it comes to about 70 dollars. Three adults and two kids work for 16 hours to harvest 70 dollars' worth of potatoes! My brother, who makes about $30 an hour in Amsterdam, figures that we each earned about 88 cents per hour in the last two days. And this doesn't include all the planting, hoeing, weeding for the whole summer. I realize that I have crossed over into the American way of thinking when I do this calculation. We explain to my dad that it is much easier for us to give him a hundred dollars to buy potatoes instead of growing them, but he says it's not about the money.

I'm no longer a little Ukrainian girl who does her parents' bidding and helps with the potato harvest without questioning if it's profitable. I ask my dad why he keeps planting potatoes every year when it isn't economically profitable, and he answers, "Доцю, *Dotsiu*, (Daughter, potatoes are second bread.)"

The first bread is made out of wheat. And it is actually wheat, not a plastic bag of preservatives, chemicals, and other additives to extend its shelf life. Ukrainian bread goes stale in three days. There is no warning label on the bag that says, "This bread may contain wheat," because people expect wheat bread to contain wheat. And also, bread doesn't come in a bag in 1999. You just carry it under your armpit. Rob remembers being in Ukraine in 1999, observing my dad buying bread off a street vendor with no plastic wrapper and no option for "how would you like it sliced?" My dad throws it in the back window of the car, comes home, takes it out, and holds it against his chest to cut a big chunk off with a knife toward his throat and enjoys it as a snack occasionally with salo and onion.

Potatoes are the second bread because people depend on potatoes as the main staple of their meal. The reason is simple: they are cheap. When I first came to the States, I immediately noticed a variety of food and I contrasted that with the diet of "bread and potatoes" I grew up with. I saw how Americans can afford a huge piece of steak on a plate and serve a small dollop of potatoes with beans as a hint to "eat your veggies." In Ukraine, it's reversed: Eat your veggies, and if you are rich, there might be a little meat. I never eat steak in Ukraine and don't feel particularly deprived because I'm not into red meat that much. I'm more into chicken drumsticks and chicken feet.

Rob asks me if we really eat chicken feet, and I look at him and say, "Yes." It's no big deal in Ukraine. So he asks me, jokingly, "So you just cut the feet off a chicken and eat them?" To which I respond, "No, we put them in soup. You just need to cook them longer. So put them in early before the potatoes and buckwheat."

He asks, "How can you eat chicken feet? Aren't they hard, like eating toenails?"

I answer, "Silly. Chickens don't have toes. But, we cut off the claws."

And there you have it.

Potato growers barter potatoes for watermelons or other unique fruits that are hard to grow. Can you imagine having a root cellar full of watermelons, like twenty of them? We do. You can eat a whole watermelon every day! You have to get your fill of watermelon in the summer because we don't have trucks driving around the neighborhood bartering watermelons for potatoes in January when it's negative 30.

But the biggest reason many generations of Ukrainians living on farms plant potatoes and don't just buy them is because the cycle of planting, weeding, and harvesting them creates the rhythm by which they live their lives. My parents did, my parents' parents did, and their parents did as well. Generations before them did it, and generations after will continue to do so. As long as Ukrainians breathe and own a piece of land, they will plant and harvest potatoes, even if it's not economically profitable.

Summer Feeds Winter Літо зиму годує

It is summertime of my childhood years. My family never takes vacations. We take some breaks to go down to the river to swim when we're done with potatoes. We are born to work and help each other. I don't remember having to make room for "quality time" or slowing down to enjoy a family meal together and having long conversations (unless it was after a long day's work and we just crashed). Except for winter, we eat to get more energy to be more productive workers. I don't know if it is the Communist idea, or that the potato fields require constant care. We don't live to eat. We eat to live. In an agrarian culture, we exist to care for the fields because those fields feed us. My dad explains the consequences of summer laziness through proverbs about summer feeding winter and that if we want to eat in the winter, we have to work hard in the summer. As children, we are not impressed with the wisdom of proverbs and we complain about the hard work. More proverbs and folk wisdom are passed on to us to teach us the importance of working hard in the summer so we would have plenty in the winter. The best teachers of the value of hard work are my parents, not through their proverbs, but through their actions. Dad never complains of rising with the rooster. He knows that constant work is his entire life.

In the U.S., I hear the term to describe our way of living life as "sustainable farming." It's such a fancy technical term for something so mundane and habitual where I'm from. Psychology explains this as follows: humans, in the process of trying to make sense of others by putting people into their own pre-existing categories, labeling Ukrainians as "sustainable farmers." In Ukraine, we don't consider ourselves "sustainable farmers" or even "farmers." We just live and grow our food on our own land.

In the future, Ukrainian farmland will be re-privatized after the fall of the Soviet empire, but for now, our village has a *kolhosp*, a collective farm that belongs to the government, complete with tractors, combines, and laborers. But common folk just have a field and some animals because that's how Ukrainians have existed for thousands of years, as an agrarian society.

To the Americans who call us "sustainable farmers," I have a hard time answering the question of whether I grew up on the farm because we don't see ourselves that way. So, subscribing to someone else's label is something I have to live with. And just because we lived off of our land, does not mean that my dad was technically a farmer. He was a civil engineer. He was a skilled architect who managed major construction projects for the government. Everyone worked for the government in those days. And everyone in the village owned a field, so, I guess, everyone was a farmer.

Ukrainian Spring Pastime: Snowdrops and *Prolisky*

Ukrainians have a deep connection with the woods. The woods offer us something different for each season. The spring forests give us the first spring wildflowers. The fall forests are rich with mushrooms. The summer forest is a good time to cool off in the shade and gather wood. But in winter, the forest sleeps. To me, woods have always been magical in the spring. After a long winter, the forest awakens and before the snow melts, it's full

of snowdrops and *pro-lisky*, known as Siberian Squill in English, but that flower name doesn't connote the same memories, smells, and feelings. So much gets lost in translation.

Snowdrops appear when the snow is still on the ground and they disappear as fast as the spring melting snow. They are considered more rare and special. We rush to the

My cousin's daughter Inna with a bouquet of prolisky, Spring 2019.

29

woods to make sure we see them before they are gone. We pick a couple of bunches and bring them home. The woods belong to everyone. You don't need to have a license for picking snowdrops. They smell of spring and newness and hope. *Prolisky* follow snowdrops and appear in mid-March. They last a little longer. It's a tradition to gather flowers and bring them home. It's like bringing a piece of the forest home with you, and with it, a piece of hope that spring is coming.

Fall is the season of picking mushrooms. Every time I smell wet leaves, I am transported to the woods where we go mushroom picking. My aunt knows where to find them and which ones to pick. My mom knows how to cook them. Some mushroom harvests are so bountiful, we pickle and can mushrooms for the winter. My favorites are *openky* and *lysychky*. To experience fall in Ukraine fully, one has to go mushroom picking.

My husband observes that Ukrainians are more in touch with nature than most Americans. Ukrainians are outdoors more often, work in the fields with their hands more, get their hands dirty without carrying sanitizers, and enjoy the fruit of the earth straight from the tree or the field more than most Americans. Ukrainians don't have to create "farm to table" programs or farmers markets. Maybe, in this one sense, America wants to be more like Ukraine?

CHAPTER 2

"How Did You Survive the Soviet Union?"

Octobryonok and Young Pioneers

I was born in 1973. The year now is 1982. These are the Brezhnev years. I am in second grade when Brezhnev dies, and it is lunchtime in school. At least once a week we are served mashed potatoes and herring and today is the mashed potatoes and herring day (sorry to make you drool). The teachers make an announcement about his death and tell us to cry for the loss of our great leader. I know that wailing clears the passage into the afterlife for the dead, so I join others because I know comrade Brezhnev could use all the help he can get. Crocodile tears run down my cheeks and into the slimy gray herring and the blue-ish mashed potatoes, diluting the already watery mound of mush. The world around me mourns the death of the General Secretary on this sad day in Soviet history.

I'll always remember this day, similar to how Americans remember where they were when Kennedy was shot. The loss is so profound, you remember where you were and what you were doing. Soviet leaders wear black in public. The state declares a five-day mourning period and we aren't allowed to laugh and be happy. The TV stations preempt all *трансляцію* (previously scheduled programming) of major shows. I can't watch my favorite animated show *Ну, погоди!* (my attempt at translation comes close to "Watch out!"), about a mean wolf chasing a bunny, but the bunny always outsmarts the wolf and runs away. (It's our version of Tom and Jerry, I later discover). We are not allowed to watch my other favorite animated cartoon *Crocodil Gena and Cheburashka*. We are to grieve the passing of our leader, the General Secretary. We don't call our leaders presidents because that's an American word and we don't emulate the evil empire. We use the term that basically means a glorified secretary.

I hear a teacher reprimanding us for exhibiting happiness. *"Не можна посміхатися!"* ("It's not permitted to smile"), she scolds us. All I remember about Brezhnev are his eyebrows, that he was overweight and moved slowly, and the very slow wave he gives from the podium during the Congress of the Communist Party of the Soviet Union. The congresses are held every five years for all the Soviet leaders to gather in Moscow and remind each other why communism is worth pursuing, even as they know that it can't sustain itself. We watch these Soviet congresses on TV as a family, almost like how American families gather to watch the Super Bowl, to see communism glorified and tanks rolled out on the streets of Moscow. But we don't have any Doritos, nachos, or pizza. Instead, there is vodka, pickles, sausage, and pickle juice as a cure for the hangover the next day.

I am an *Octobryonok* (*жовтеня Zhovtenya* in Ukrainian), a member of a youth organization. *Octobryonok* means "October child" because October was the month of the Russian Revolution in 1917, so we become the "children of the revolution," charged with carrying the proletariat ideas forward. Children in the United States have organizations to join, like the Brownies and Webeloes, and then they can work their way up to the Girl Scouts and Boy Scouts, and then on up to the Democratic or Republican parties. Well, we have the same thing, but instead of learning how to sell cookies or build a fire in the rain, we learn how to be good communists.

Myself, age 7 as an Octobryonok wearing a pin with a young Lenin.

Becoming an *Octobryonok* is the first step in the promotion toward Communist Party membership. This step is for children in elementary school. I have to wear a special pin with Lenin's face engraved in it. Heaven forbid, you forget to wear the pin on your uniform.

The uniforms are spotless. Girls wear a black dress with white removable collars and cuffs for the sleeves, which are supposed to be washed, pressed, and resewn back on weekly. I wash mine in the sink with hand soap, dry them on the radiator, and sew them back on every single week. If I forget to do it the night before, my mom teaches me how to wash it and dry it with a hot iron in the morning. But it makes the collars damp and I go to school with a clean, pressed white collar that feels wet on my neck.

In 1985 I am in fifth grade and *Octobryonoks* are promoted to join the Young Pioneers. It is an exciting moment! We wear a bright red *galstook* (a triangular silk kerchief tied around our necks with a particular knot, and the knot has to be done just right and not sloppy). Similar to the white cuffs on the uniform, the *galstook* also has to be washed and pressed regularly. But because it is tied around our necks and we don't take daily showers, we have to wash and press it every other day. On some days, I don't listen to Mom and hang my *galstook* on the hot radiator and discover the next morning that I can't iron out the humps in the silk. I spray some water on it to make it damp, iron it and hear my girlfriend Luda calling me outside, "Hurry up! We'll be late for school!"

The youth of the Soviet Union don't get a traditional education during the communist era. We get indoctrination and brainwashing. We are raised nationalists to the core, taught to love our *Родина Мать* (Motherland), our Party, and the Glorious Communist Future. The party is Communist, but we never achieve communism. We only have communist-flavored socialism. I don't know the difference between the two and we don't dare ask any questions. We firmly believe in our leaders to lead us to a bright future. We are taught how to respect our elders, to give up our seat on the bus for the elderly, and to help elderly women cross the street. We are taught to be polite, well-behaved children and because of that, I love my teachers and everything they offer.

The brainwashing starts when we first learn how to read. My first reader starts with a portrait of Lenin and a short poem to inspire us to be like him. The content of the book is all propaganda: how great the Soviet Union is, how great Lenin is, and how great our communist future will be.

Picture of a young Lenin walking to school from our first reader, 1985. Publisher: Soviet School.

(The translation on the page above is as follows: *Everything starts in life with a small thing: from the kernel comes bread, and from a small ray of light comes a star. And even Lenin started his difficult life with the First Reader*).

Even in my German language classes, we use the Grammar Translation learning method by reading, translating, and memorizing biographies of German socialists, like Clara Zetkin, a Marxist theorist who was an activist for women's rights and an active member of the Social Democratic Party of Germany.

Our behavior also has to be in line with the Party orders. When raising your hand, it has to be at 90 degrees, perpendicular to the left hand. If you stretch out your hand into the air above your head, you will never be called on by the teacher. You are violating Party orders, and you are not being a good Octobryonok or a Young Pioneer.

As an adult, I still have a knee-jerk reaction when I want to raise my hand at a meeting and I feel like I'm violating the Party orders by not holding my arm at a right angle. I think I have a slight version of PTSD. (Do they provide therapy for communist-based PTSD? If not, maybe I should start my own private practice support group.)

At about age 15, members of the Young Pioneers are promoted to the Youth Communist League. We have to pass an exam to be accepted. It is the highest honor for a Soviet teenager to be a member. The Young Pioneers have a special salute—a raised arm at an angle in front of their face. It is like a military salute but your hand goes across your forehead. Wearing our red *galstooks* and our pressed uniforms, we salute the Communist Party at the beginning of the school day and sing the Soviet national anthem about how great our union is, comprised of 15 free republics.

Here is a translation of the anthem of the Union of Soviet Socialist Republics:

Unbreakable union of free republics
Welded forever great Rus'
Long live the creation of the people's work
United, mighty Soviet Union.

Hail the fatherland, our free one,
A reliable fortress of people's friendships!
Party of Lenin—the strength of the people,
Communism leads us to triumph!

Through storms shone the light of freedom,
And great Lenin illuminated our path,

35

To the right cause, he raised up the people,
He inspired us to work and progress!

With the victory of immortal communist ideals
We see the future of our country,
To the red banner of our sacred fatherland
We will forever be wholeheartedly true!

The Soviet anthem was written to express the pride of being part of such a great union, but most republics had been forced to join the republic at the end of a rifle barrel, and the idea of "free" republics being welded together was an odious thought. But as children, we don't know this. We just wear our uniforms and sing the song they tell us to. This production is a combination of Kafka, Orwell, and mass marketing.

Assembling an AK-47 Blindfolded ... in Eighth Grade

In 1988 the space shuttle Challenger explodes on lift-off, Halley's comet pays the Earth a visit, Chernobyl blows its top, American audiences flock to see *Top Gun*, and I am training to fire automatic weapons.

I am in eighth grade. As a child who lives through the last decades of communism, my public education includes learning how to disassemble, clean, and re-assemble an AK-47 blindfolded. Now, as I write this, I still have some muscle memory for how it is done, how to properly seat the magazine into the receiver extension assembly, and how to thread the carrier spring through the hole at the top of the barrel. Girls are included in this training instead of being sent off to Home Economics class to learn to sew kitchen aprons. I am quite handy with the Kalashnikov. This is mandatory training, part of our civics class.

Back in the day when Americans had civics classes, they had to learn how to say the Pledge of Allegiance to the flag, sing the national anthem, and how to be good citizens. In the USSR, we learn how to shoot AK-47s and pull on and off our gas masks. I absolutely hate doing this because the masks have to be airtight to work properly and I can't get it over my head. I have a fear of suffocating when trying to pull that thick, stinky, dirty rubber mask over my head. During this exercise, I wouldn't mind going to sew aprons in Home Ec., but we don't have that option. We have to make sure we are ready in case of an impending air strike from the Americans.

Our civics teacher, who is a former military officer, makes us march around the school in gas masks. Being forced to march in these hot masks, through which I can barely see or breathe, is torture. As a reprieve from this misery, we are then allowed to go shoot automatic weapons at the shooting range 20 meters away from the track where fifth graders are running laps during gym class. There is also a playground and a school garden next to the range, but the bullets supposedly aren't a threat to anyone because the shooting range is in a deep ravine. In the U.S., you have to drive out into the country to find a shooting range, but in the USSR, shooting machine guns is all part of fun and games.

As elementary schoolchildren, we fear for our lives when our teachers show us pictures of big mushroom clouds from an atomic bomb and we worry that Americans might push the button at any minute. We practice putting on masks made out of cheesecloth and elastic straps and hide under our desks. As a second grader, I'm not very good at fitting the masks on and feel terrified that I might die because of my inability to navigate the straps. How do our teachers possibly think that a flimsy cheesecloth mask is going to save us from radioactive dust? We don't rehearse for a nuclear attack with gas masks until high school.

What Do Jeans Have to Do with Communism?

I grew up with two siblings: my sister Alla, who was four and a half years older than me, and my brother Bogdan, who was eight years younger than me. The difference in years between my sister and my brother was fifteen years. I was in first grade when Bogdan was born. We were so excited when he came home that I ran over and told Luda that I have a baby brother! My sister and I treated him like he was a "live toy": he was so cute to play with! But it wasn't as easy to dress him as it was dressing our dolls.

He was the first boy after two girls. His name Bog-dan literally means God-given. Our grandpa Ivan recommended that name to my parents because Bogdan was truly a gift from God. He was very special and we all loved him. When he started walking, he would hang out with Dad in his garage. Dad finally got his little helper, because Mom has had two helpers all these years.

It was my responsibility to care for my brother and take him with me when I played with friends. I changed and washed his cloth diapers. We were so ahead of our time with the cloth diapers! Later in Minnesota when my kids were born, I met some moms who used cloth diapers, but I used Pampers. I didn't want to tell them that I'd had my share of wash-ing cloth dia-pers back in the early 80's in the river, called Rotten Running Water (Hnyliy Tikych). As my brother grew up, our lives

My sister Alla at Bethel University during her visit for chemo treatment in the spring of 1999.

separated more and more and due to a nine-year age difference, our friends and our activities were different. Bogdan recently told me, "Because we were born nine years apart, we had very different lives, even growing up under the same roof." Despite these differences, Bogdan reminds me so much of Alla, especially in terms of personality and character.

This portion of this chapter will be about my sister. It is another one of those bittersweet chapters in my life and in my book because she died from lung cancer at the age of 31. She died on my birthday. This chapter is dedicated to her.

The year is 1983. It's springtime. Alla is in eighth grade. I'm in third grade. Alla is shy. I am the outgoing one. Alla is obedient. I am rebellious. Alla is meticulous. I am expedient. Alla is quiet. I am demanding. Alla is laid back. Our polarized personalities play out when my sister finds out that my mom's store gets a new shipment of clothes, including a rare, foreign, highly sought-after item: a pair of American jeans.

My mom works in retail. Before this, she worked in a bookstore, a shoe store (which was next to the bookstore), and a fabric and clothing store. Mom brings home Mark Twain's *The Adventure of Tom Sawyer*, Oscar Wilde's *The Picture of Dorian Gray*, Victor Hugo's *Les Misérables*, and Giovanni Boccaccio's *The Decameron*. I'm still amazed at how we had access to those because that's close to reading heresy according to the Soviet ideology. Hugo was legit because he also critiqued the bourgeoisie. Not sure how *The Decameron* passed the Soviet test.

These are the glorious Brezhnev years and the Soviet Union is leading us toward a bright shiny future following in the footsteps of our great Lenin. The stores' inventories consist of things made only in the Soviet Union. Because all forms of production and manufacturing in the USSR are government-owned, clothing and tractors and dishes and underwear come with a label that says, "made in the USSR" or more specifically, "made in Belarus" or "made in Uzbekistan."

When I come to the U.S. and I see a big truck with Procter & Gamble or Johnson & Johnson written in big letters all over the truck, I realize that Procter & Gamble are two different people and that people actually own businesses and they have income from their businesses versus giving all their money to the government. People-owned businesses are unheard of in communist times because, "everything belongs to people," as Brezhnev said. All I know is that everything belongs to the government. All the production is government-owned and government-regulated. There is no competition and no incentive to be creative and come up with ideas like ziplock bags and Kleenex. So, while the Americans are inventing sliced bread and superheroes, the Soviets are developing our space program. We don't have any energy left over for competition and creativity for such mundane things as plastic bags, because all of our energy goes into more important things, like competing with the Americans to see who will get into space first. We win in space, sending the first man into orbit, but lose in daily conveniences. That's my explanation for why I haven't grown up with ziplock bags for my school sandwiches or toilet paper. I wrap my sandwiches in newspaper and later use the same newspaper in the bathroom. It also provides great reading material while you are squatting. We rip up the Communist Truth and hang it on a nail and use it for wiping our behinds. In my "educated" opinion now, it was the best use for it.

During my school years in the 1980s, our "wonderful" Soviet government wants to protect us from Western influences that come via American jeans and down jackets with bright colors versus shades of gray (we also have fifty shades of gray, found in our suit jackets, coats, mittens, and pants). Seeing bright green or yellow jackets means you are a foreign tourist. (See later chapter about Rob showing up in post-Soviet Ukraine looking like a bumblebee in his black and yellow North Face jacket. Can you visualize it?)

With this description of how limited the wares are at our local village "boutiques," you can imagine what a rare treat it is for us to have American jeans. When my sister discovers that Mom has a pair of American jeans in her store, she asks, "Ru, ask Mom to get me a pair of jeans. I need them so I can be cool." My sister is in the ninth grade. She is always a very stylish dresser. Also, she tells me she is dating a guy she really likes, so she desperately needs those jeans to impress him. Because Brezhnev and his cabinet work very hard to protect us from foreign pollution, those jeans aren't sold *на прилавці* (in the open), you can only buy them *під столом* (under the table), sort of like an English equivalent of "on the black market," but that equivalent doesn't really work. There are no other markets in the village.

I guess the black market is not a physical market but a metaphorical market. The jeans are smuggled past Customs somewhere to my mom's store but are sold illegally. The prices on those foreign items are arbitrary; the managers ask whatever price they want. Because of my mom's position at the store, she is often able to bring home special items that other families can't get. For example, one time she brings home a bright red Japanese down jacket, light as a feather. Then she presents me with shiny, red Italian shoes with a strap around the ankle, made of real Italian leather, but they are one size too small for me. I tell my mom that my toes don't hurt (because they are numb, I can't feel them anymore), but she takes them back the next day. Then she brings home a special pair of velcro brown shoes, and I think that is the best invention since sliced bread. Wait, there is no sliced bread in the '70s and '80s. It will be a 21st-century invention.

I approach my mom and boldly ask her (the only way I talk) for the jeans on Alla's behalf, but she says they are too expensive. So I beg her again nicely, promising that I'd hoe all the potato fields by myself. She finally gives in and soon afterward the jeans arrive. She pays about 100 rubles for them, which is half of her paycheck for that month. My sister and I smell the jeans and talk about how someone said that American jeans were soaked in camel urine. The jeans even smell foreign, not like our Soviet dungarees covered in factory dust, but more exotic. Even camel urine smells exotic to us. Then we notice the rivets. The rivets are copper color and say the same thing on each one: Gold Star, Gold Star … Gold Star everywhere. We have never seen anything like that. The only brand we know is "Made in the USSR." We have no brands or trademarks on our products, mostly because we have no private companies.

We admire the jeans again. They are dark blue, made with a very thick and sturdy denim. Alla wears them to school the next day and on all of her dates. She is my cool big sister. I miss her as I recount these memories because she is gone. I can't call her and ask her if I got the details right. I can't laugh with her sharing these memories and telling her that she is in my memoir. She died at the age of 31 from adenocarcinoma of the lungs.

The Soviet propaganda machine fills televisions with government-produced programming that shows American homeless people on the news, telling us that this is what rotten capitalism does to people: it makes them homeless. But to our great surprise, the homeless people are wearing JEANS!

CHAPTER 3

"How Do You Celebrate Thanksgiving in Ukraine?"

B efore I answer the question about our Thanksgiving traditions (believe it or not, people did ask me several times how we celebrate American Thanksgiving, as if the Pilgrims landed on the Crimean peninsula and were greeted by Cossacks), I have to share about the holidays and celebrations I grew up with in the '70s and '80s and how they were observed. Below is a list of the major holidays observed during the Soviet calendar and other significant events.

New Year's, January 1st

Christmas Eve, January 6th

Christmas Day, January 7th

Old New Year, January 14th

February 23th, Red Army Day

March 8th, International Women's Day

Easter

May 1st, May Day

May 9th, Victory Day

September 1st, Knowledge Day - First Bell (First Day of School)

May 25th, Last Bell (Last Day of School)

Birthdays

There was no Independence Day when I was growing up because Ukraine was the Ukrainian Soviet Socialist Republic and not an independent nation.

But now, there is a new holiday for Ukrainians to celebrate on August 24th, Ukraine's Independence Day from the Soviet Union. We are independent once more! No wonder the Ukrainian national anthem is called *Ukraine's Not Dead Yet*. Can you imagine your country singing the anthem, "The USA is not dead yet," as if you're saying, "Well, yes, I'm sure we'll be dead sometime soon, but as for today, we're not dead." Let that sink in for a moment.

Since this book isn't dedicated to Ukrainian history, I can't indulge in all the details, but I will take the time to say that Ukrainians have had their share of subjugation from a variety of occupiers, including the Greeks, Scythians, Sarmato-Alan, clans of west Kazakhs, the Mongol Golden Horde, Poland, Russia, Russia, and Russia again. When I tell Rob that the Mongol Golden Rule empire lasted more than 200 years, he says, "That's long! I'm surprised you guys still exist." It feels like we are in the way of everyone who wants to rule over us or take our resources. According to American agriculturalists, Ukraine has the richest soil, *chernozem,* along with many other natural resources. Paired with its access to the Black Sea, it makes the country of Ukraine a desirable target.

The Ukrainian National Anthem—*Ukraine is Not Dead Yet*

Ukraine's glory has not yet died, nor her freedom,
Upon us, my young brothers, fate shall yet smile.
Our enemies will perish, like dew in the morning sun,
And we too shall rule, brothers, in our own land.

Refrain
Souls and bodies we'll lay down, all for our freedom,
And we will show that we, brothers, are of the Cossack nation!

New Year's

I am in fifth grade, dressed as a snowflake. My mom made this costume for me. We are getting ready for the biggest celebration of the year,

Yalinka—decorating the New Year Tree or *новорічна ялинка (novorichna yalinka)*. What Americans call a Christmas tree, we call a fir tree.

There are many stories about how the tree got the New Year name, and some of the versions include Stalin and his daughter Svetlana. The Bolsheviks had banned Christmas and Christmas trees because it was considered a bourgeois and harmful festival, making life miserable for the children of the proletariat whose families couldn't afford trees or gifts. After 18 years of a ban on Christmas, the Communist leadership decided there would be advantages to having a beautiful tree to highlight the accomplishments of the Communist Party, so they reinstituted the tradition of the tree without all of the pagan and Christian pageantry and symbolism. They shifted the celebration to take place on New Year's starting in 1935, with Pravda touting the new holiday as having "the atmosphere of fairy tale and magic." Instead of having a tree ensconced with an angel and surrounded by a manger scene, the holiday's main decorations changed considerably compared to the tsarist era. They placed a Red Star on top of the tree and had ornaments depicting Lenin and Stalin, the Space Race, Snegurochka (the Snow Maiden), and Father Frost, and other ornaments representing agriculture and cultural icons.

The tree is decorated in December for New Year's Eve on December 31st and New Year's Day. As schoolchildren, we have the celebration on the last day of school before the winter break, December 26th or 27th. We rehearse our presentation ahead of time, dress up in costumes of animals and snowflakes, and dance around our tree for our parents and teachers. In my school, the tree is in the gym. I usually dress up in a white dress with puffy white sleeves, trying to look like a snowflake, along with the other girls. Boys show up as bunnies and wolves. The kids line up on both sides, eagerly waiting for Father Frost to show up with *Снігурочка (Snigurochka,* his Snow Maiden). If he doesn't show up, we start chanting, "Father Frost, Father Frost, Father Frost!" *Snigurochka* always accompanies Father Frost, dressed in a gorgeous light blue and white dress and a spectacular crown surrounding her head with a raised point in the front. (Disney seemed to have borrowed *Snigurochka's* crown and dress for Elsa from *Frozen*.) Father Frost carries a big heavy bag with gifts and candy, and *Snigurochka* is responsible for distributing the presents.

A bag of candy is the only gift we receive on New Year's Eve, and yet we are thrilled. There are no extravagant gifts exchanged in my family. I remember my mom bringing a bag of candy in a pretty holiday bag from work that the government provides. We are happy to get candy. We don't feel deprived. I don't have a sense of entitlement, and there is no expectation to find ten presents under the tree on Christmas morning.

New Year's Eve is celebrated with a lavish dinner to say goodbye to the old year and to welcome the new. Young people and energetic adults stay up all night partying. When I arrive in the U.S., and New Year's Eve is approaching, I get excited to celebrate my first New Year in the new country with my American parents, Ron and Carol. To my dismay, I find that there is no lavish dinner in the making, no big party to attend. New Year's Eve is not a big deal in the United States for married couples who are tired and don't want to stay up until midnight. No one warns me, because I hadn't shared my expectations and they hadn't shared theirs. I offer hot cocoa to my host family to usher in the New Year at midnight, but they refuse my celebratory offer. They say that it is too late and we all just go to bed.

Christmas Eve

Christmas Eve is on January 6th because the Orthodox church follows the old Julian calendar. Christmas is a time for going house to house singing carols (called *kolyadky*) and getting candy and money from the neighbors. This tradition of singing carols is called *kolyaduvannya*. Comparing it to trick or treating on Halloween night doesn't seem respectful to me, but in my presentation in American classrooms, that's how many American kids make a connection to something they know.

Ukraine is an ancient land with many pagan traditions. *Kolyaduvannya* (caroling) is one of those pagan traditions related to the winter cycle. According to some sources, people used to sing *kolyadky* on the winter solstice on December 21st. But after Ukraine was Christianized in 988, the Orthodox Church banished pagan traditions and, as a result, Christian and pagan rituals and traditions were integrated. During the earlier days of *kolyaduvannya*, people dressed up in animal costumes and carried a big star (not a Red Star but a multipointed star resembling the sun), celebrating a mix of pagan traditions in the new Christian era.

I am 10 years old. It's January 6th, Christmas Eve, 6 p.m. It's dark and cold outside, and I'm dressed warm. I say, "Off we go!" to my parents when leaving the house. My friends and I are about to go from house to house singing carols. I think my sister already left because she is five years older than me and she goes caroling with her friends. I come to the first neighbor's house and sing my favorite carol:

Добрий вечір тобі, пане господарю, радуйся!
Dobriy vechir tobi, paneh hospodaryi, raduisya!
"Good evening to you, master, rejoice!"

My friends join me and we sing more carols. The neighbor gives us candy, walnuts, and a few coins. We go from house to house singing many different kinds of *kolyadki* getting more candy, money, and nuts. The last house we visit is my grandparents' house. My grandpa picks me up, puts me on his lap and gives me money. He is always generous with his grandkids and we each get a paper ruble (currency at the time).

We return from *kolyaduvannya* and eat *kutia*. *Kutia* is a ceremonial grain dish enjoyed only on Christmas Eve, once a year. It is a wheat berry mix with raisins, ground poppy seeds, and honey in milk or dried fruit compote. Even though it's a sweet meal, we are allowed to eat it as the first meal of the Christmas dinner. After *kutia*, we eat other special holiday foods: pork cutlets, homemade sausage from the pig we butchered earlier in December, cabbage rolls, *kholodets* (aspic), vinaigrette salad, pickled tomatoes, and cucumbers. My sister runs to the root cellar to get some canned apples in a sugary syrup. Those are for dessert. I prefer to have *horishky* cookies which Mom serves. They are walnut-shaped cookies filled with sweetened condensed caramelized milk and walnuts from our tree. I look at the brown caramelized milk and remember that it was my job to boil a can of sweetened condensed milk in a pot of water for at least three hours.

In the U.S., I forget about *kutia* for several years. Transplanted immigrants often lose something in the transition from one kitchen to the other. At least, that is the case for me. I enjoy making Christmas cookies with my American mother-in-law the first several Christmases in the U.S. and start new traditions with my family, like making calzones. People ask me about Ukrainian Christmas traditions and I don't remember any except for caroling. *Kutia* vanishes from my memory.

Then one year when my brother comes to visit me in Minnesota, he reminds me of *kutia* and I make it with him. *Kutia* reconnects us as a brother and sister. It takes me back to my childhood and I feel the warmth of the house after *kolyaduvannya* on a cold winter night. *Kutia* brings my childhood and my mom's kitchen into my new kitchen in Minnesota. I don't remember all the ingredients, but I remember two: *pshenytsia* (wheat) and poppy seeds. I discover that *pshenytsia* is translated as wheat berries in the U.S. I write the word for wheat in Ukrainian because "wheat berries" does not connote the same memories, tastes, and feelings. There is so much more meaning for me in the

My brother Bogdan and I. He surprised me with a visit on my 40th birthday when he came all the way from Amsterdam and showed up in my living room, February 16, 2014.

Ukrainian word *pshenytsia*. When I say it, I see wheat fields swaying in the wind against the azure blue sky, the two colors in our flag (blue for the sky, yellow for wheat).

Another ingredient I remember is poppy seeds. I see my mom grinding them with a mortar and pestle until the white milky substance appeared in the process. Sometimes I am given the job but my little hands tire quickly. In America, there is no mortar and pestle and I know that I don't want to grind the poppy seeds. I go to an American grocery store and discover that they carry poppy seeds in a can already ground up with raisins! I save myself three hours of time, but lose the tradition.

Even now, when I forget authentic Ukrainian cooking, I often go to Natashaskitchen.com and I find recipes for *kutia, horishky, kholodets,* and other delicacies from my childhood Christmas.

There are no celebrations on Christmas Day in Ukraine. The only people who actually celebrate Christmas are those who believe in Christ. They spend all day in church singing and celebrating Christ's birth. I know, it's a shocker, spending the whole day in church, let alone on Christmas. You can imagine the shock I have when I come to the U.S. and Christians do not go to celebrate Christ's birth on Christmas Day but spend it opening presents. When my parents visit me, I have a hard time convincing them that the presents are supposed to remind us that Christ is God's gift to the world. They look at me in disbelief, "Wow, that's quite a stretch, whatever it takes to justify materialism in America!"

So, we all get in the car and I take them to the Ukrainian Church of Evangelical Baptist Christians (the actual name) in Saint Louis Park, Minnesota, where other Christ followers celebrate Christ on Christmas Day. Radical, I know.

Old New Year's Eve

Old New Year's Eve on January 13th and the Old New Year on January 14th were not official holidays, but a carryover of the Julian calendar that was followed by the Orthodox church.

The Old New Year's Eve is also called Malanka. It's similar to Christmas Eve, which includes caroling door to door and playing pranks. The last house is a family member's home where we throw handfuls of wheat and rice grains around the entrance and inside the house. With this tradition, we bless the family with wealth, prosperity, and health. That's the day the song *Щедрик (Schedryk)*, known in the U.S. as the *Carol of the Bells*, was written for. *Schedryk* means the "Generous One" or the "Bountiful One" and wishes people prosperity for the new year. It has absolutely no connection to Christmas whatsoever, until it was translated into English with "Christmas is here, bringing good cheer ..."

Щедрик (*Shchedryk*)	Bountiful
In Ukrainian	*In English*
Щедрик щедрик,	Bountiful, bountiful,
Щедрівочка,	New Year's Carol.
прилетіла ластівочка,	A little swallow flew in
стала собі щебетати,	And started twittering
господаря викликати:	To call the master,
"Вийди, вийди, господарю,	"Come out, come out, master,
подивися на кошару,	Look at the sheep pen,
там овечки покотились,	There the lambs nestle,
а ягнички народились.	And lambkins were born.
В тебе товар весь хороший,	Since you have all good livestock,
будеш мати мірку грошей,	You shall have a lot of money.
В тебе товар весь хороший,	Since you have all good livestock,
будеш мати мірку грошей,	You shall have a lot of money,
хоч не грошей, то полова:	If not money, then chaff:

50

в тебе жінка чорноброва.	You have a beautiful dark-browed wife.
Щедрик щедрик,	Bountiful, bountiful,
Щедрівочка,	New Year's Carol,
прилетіла ластівочка.	A little swallow flew in.

Go ahead and try singing it to the tune of *The Carol of the Bells*.

However, I don't remember ever singing this song personally. I bet the Soviet government didn't like it and stopped playing it. They tried to get rid of Ukrainian literature, music, language, poetry, and art to erase our identity. As the proverb goes, "They wanted to bury us. But they forgot that we were seeds."

The other holidays described below, celebrated in the '70s and '80s fashion, had three themes in common: showing off with military parades, giving glory to the Party (not like a party with confetti, but the Communist Party), adults getting drunk, and kids playing with balloons.

Soviet Army and Navy Day

"Dad, look what I made for you!" I proudly show dad a white cloth napkin I embroidered for him with a tank and a carnation on it, the flower of the Revolution and the Soviet Army. He is not impressed or touched. Dad didn't serve in the army and a napkin with a tank doesn't mean much to him, but he smiles and shows his appreciation for the thought behind it.

День Советской Армии и Военно-Морского флота or Soviet Army and Navy Day is the day to celebrate our men, especially the glorious Soviet Army and Navy. At some point, it is renamed as Men's Day *(День Мужчин)*, like, you know, Monday, Tuesday, Mensday... Army service is compulsory in Ukraine. Even my brother was almost drafted to fight the Russian "peacemakers" when they invaded Eastern Ukraine in 2014.

(Only in an Orwellian state like Russia would invading forces be called "peacemakers.")

Each boy at the age of 18 is drafted to serve in the army. It is an important tradition to have a special girl there to send them off to boot camp with a huge party and a lot of drinking. I am appointed to be the girl to send off my neighbor who I dated for a short time. In the U.S., a boy asks a girl to go to prom with him. In Ukraine, a girl is asked to send a boy off to war.

March 8th ~ International Women's Day

It's a sunny warm day at the beginning of March 1993. I'm in Cherkassy, home to my college, Bohdan Khmelnytsky University. I'm walking back to my dorm from the bus stop, returning from downtown. The city side-walks are full of flower stands with people selling roses, tulips, *prolisky,* and snowdrops. All around I see women dressed up in their nicest skirts and blouses, wearing high heels, with their coats swung open. The melting snow slowly makes its way to the Dnieper River, and I jump over a puddle to avoid getting my new heels wet and dirty. I am holding a bouquet of tulips presented to me from some guy on the street simply because it's Woman's Day or *Жіночий День.* Tulips become my favorite flowers because of the fond memories of this holiday. My mom's flower bed is full of tulips in the spring.

March 8th is a holiday set aside to celebrate working women of the world. Clara Zetkin, whose biography we studied in my German language classes, was a Marxist theorist, a women's rights activist, and the founder of the holiday back in 1909. Her conception behind Women's Day was with a focus on women's rights and suffrage.

In Ukraine, the holiday is celebrated by bringing flowers to all the women in your life—mothers, wives, sisters, and daughters—to honor and pamper them. The holiday has become less about highlighting the need for women's rights and more about making women happy by wishing them "womanly happiness," which means to preserve one's youthful figure, land a good husband, and excel at motherhood. It is not about women pursuing their dreams, having equal pay and equal rights, or being free from sexual harassment at work and public places, and free from domestic abuse. It isn't necessarily about a Rosie-the-Riveter kind of women's holiday, nor an "All Feminists Unite!" rally, but more about women being pampered by their husbands spending money on gifts and pouring love on them. It is exhausting for the guys, that's for sure. Even young girls get flowers from boys in school.

I make sure to tell Rob that Women's Day is a big deal in Ukraine. I particularly stress the pampering and the flowers part. But the funniest thing is … I forget to tell him there is also a Men's Day. For years, every time Women's Day rolls around, I remind Rob to get me flowers and treat me like a princess. He takes me out to dinner with my other female friends from the former Soviet Union to a Russian restaurant called Moscow on the Hill in St. Paul, and we all celebrate together, eating *vareniky, cutletky,* and *olivye* salad.

After ten years of celebrations, one of my friends asks Rob how we celebrate Men's Day. He looks at me and asked incredulously, "There's a Men's Day?" I just look back at him sheepishly and say, "Oh, I forgot." He responds, "Wait. After all these years of celebrating Women's Day, now you tell me there's been a Men's Day all along? And you just conveniently forget?" I give him some excuse about us not celebrating that day much in our family, but I don't think he believes me. Nobody remembers either February 23rd or March 8th in my house, because we don't celebrate them in the U.S.

Easter

It's the day before Easter, 1991. My sister and I help mom boil the eggs in onion skins, beet juice, and other natural colors. We realize we are going to end up with only three colors. Mom decides to buy some "non-natural" dyes so we can have a more festive plate with more colorful eggs for Easter.

We make pink, azure, purple, deep red, bright yellow, and orange eggs. We buy *paska*, a very traditional Easter bread, and arrange the eggs around the bread on the table. The main centerpiece of our Easter dinner is the *paska*. I admire the cylindrical shape of *paska* before it gets cut and contrast it with the common rectangular bread we eat every day. *Paska* is only consumed on Easter. It's not your average sweet bread you might eat for dessert. It is definitely something special.

Paska Recipe:

3 cups bread flour
½ tsp salt
½ cup sugar
Grated rind from ½ orange and ½ lemon
½ tsp vanilla
¼ cup orange juice
4 egg yolks, 1 egg whites, beat lightly
½ cup boiled and cooled milk
¼ cup butter
1 Tbsp yeast
¼ cup raisins

Paska: Ukrainian Easter Bread

It's Easter dinner the next day, but before we dig into our festive dinner, we play this game of knocking our eggs against each other's to see whose is the strongest. I often beat my sister, strategically cracking her egg, but then she carefully inspects her egg and hits mine and breaks it. We do this for a few more rounds, maybe four or five eggs each. We know we are supposed to eat those eggs, and I realize we eat more eggs in one day than in the entire month. The colors are so bright. I want to eat them all. But I reach for pork cutlets, cabbage rolls, meat rolls, pieces of *buzhanina* (specially cured and prepared pork meat), and a salad.

To make a tall cylindrical paska, I bake it in a coffee can (Folgers can will do). Prepare the can by removing the label from the outside, and the rim at the top of the can. Make the dough in your bread machine or by hand. Baste the dough with egg yolk with 1 tablespoon water. Spray the can with oil to prevent sticking. Bake the paska at 350 degrees for 40 minutes. Watch for the top to turn golden brown, then cover it with aluminum foil and continue baking for another 20 minutes. Take the bread out of the can immediately to prevent water condensation inside the can. When cooled, drizzle the paska with frosting (¼ cup powdered sugar and a teaspoon of water). Your house should smell like vanilla and orange peel.

The most devoted Orthodox Christians go to church only twice a year, on Christmas and Easter. The devout take a basket of boiled eggs and paska bread for the priest to bless. I don't grow up with the tradition of having eggs blessed, which has something to do with fertility, but I do enjoy having our Easter egg battles with my sister or cousins. In my family and throughout the entire region, making Easter eggs never involves hot wax and *kistka*, a tool for drawing intricate designs on raw eggshells. Those are called *pysanky,* from the word *pysaty* which means "to write" because you literally write with a tool filled with hot wax on a raw eggshell. It is a tradition of Western Ukrainians, who are the keepers of ancient Ukrainian traditions and customs.

I'm in Pinewood Elementary School in Anoka, Minnesota, in 1996, and I am upholding my duty to represent Ukraine with dignity. There is an expectation by my fellow teachers that I know how to make *pysanky* and I am asked to teach that art to fifth graders. I study the meanings and the symbolism behind the intricate lines, figures, and designs that are drawn on the egg. I am excited to teach young American schoolchildren centuries-old tradition. I learn that triangles stand for air, water, and fire. Ribbons symbolize everlasting life. Poppies are a beloved Ukrainian art motif and stand for joy and beauty. The sun and stars are the symbols of life, fortune, and growth.

I rise to the challenge to figure out how to make Ukrainian Easter eggs pass on a great national tradition ... that I never grew up with. I buy all the supplies, including the *kistkas*, the wax, the dyes, the drying rack, a book with instructions and explanations of the symbolism behind the designs, and an instructional video. To my surprise, I learn how to make Ukrainian Easter eggs from a Norwegian woman who is married to a Ukrainian guy (I think they are related to the owners of Kramarchuk Sausage Company, which is a famous Eastern European deli and restaurant in Minneapolis).

I teach Ukrainian Easter egg design to fifth graders, who I discover are not very interested in the meanings of the ancient pagan origins of the lines we draw on the egg with melted wax. They draw skulls, stick figures fighting, and their favorite football team's mascot. For them, the practice of egg designs is not about honoring a sacred centuries-old tradition that has symbolism behind every line, but an exercise in free-flowing creativity with no attention to linear precision or upholding the traditions of old. I'm reminded that in American schools, art is about self-expression, not about copying designs I place in front of them to emulate. I can't force them to cherish an old tradition and retain its original meanings. They put their own meanings into this practice.

In contrast with American Easter, there are no Easter bunnies in our Ukrainian villages, and no grown-ups hiding eggs in the grass for us to find. Even though Easter didn't mean anything to me as a child, when I opened my heart to Christ, Easter became an opportunity to celebrate my resurrected Savior. My biggest challenge in parenting my own children is switching over to the American way of doing Easter, which always involves plastic Easter eggs in colorful baskets, chocolate, and adults wearing big bunny costumes. I'm glad we also take a little time to remember that Christ rose on Easter, but I notice that kids get more excited about the bunny than the resurrected Jesus. Why is it easier to believe in the Easter Bunny than Jesus? Maybe because they can physically see and hug the bunny at the mall or even at church, just some guy dressed in a fluffy costume with big floppy ears. Blessed are those who believe without seeing! Jesus, I mean, not the Easter Bunny.

It's 2019. My first Easter without Mom. I miss hearing my mom say,

"Христос Воскрес! "Christ is Risen!,"
"Воістину Воскрес! "He is Risen indeed," I reply

"Христос Воскрес! "Christ is Risen!"
"Воістину Воскрес! "He is Risen indeed." I reply

She says it a third time, following the age-old tradition.
"Христос Воскрес! Christ is Risen!"
"Воістину Воскрес! He is Risen indeed."

I make paska the day before Easter Sunday. I display my paska on the dinner table and my tears well up because I can't show her my creation. She is not here to tell me, "I'm so proud of you. It looks beautiful. I buy mine at the store. It's too much work to make it from scratch. I don't have the energy anymore."

May 1st - May Day

May Day brings up many memories for me, all involving big parades, but not like your 4th of July parade. Our parades were mandatory. All the schoolkids, teachers, and other community members gather at the school and walk down the street holding banners and balloons marching behind a big band playing Soviet military music and leading the way to the center of town. We are forced to stand there throughout the inevitable motivational speech about the glorious communist future. All the students are dressed up in their school uniforms. Girls are wearing white aprons over black dresses, with neatly pressed white collars and big bows in their hair, while the boys are decked out in suit jackets.

After the parade, the families go into the woods or parks, spread a blanket out on the grass, and have a picnic. Some comrades go into the woods because there are no parks in the town where I grew up. I hear a lot of alcohol is consumed by adults at their May Day picnics.

May 9th - Victory Day

Every March 9th we commemorate the day that the Nazis signed the Instrument of Surrender, ending the Great Patriotic War, or World War II as it is called in America. Like May Day, Victory Day also involves parades that honor World War II veterans. They are placed at the front of the parade, with the school and local community following. We all walk to the center of the village and lay wreaths by the Tomb of the Unknown Soldier. Each village and town in Ukraine has a WWII memorial because the Nazis marched through all of Ukraine, including my hometown, but were defeated in the Battle of Stalingrad where the Germans were encircled and defeated. When Americans tell me that they won World War II, Ukrainians have a hard time swallowing this because we lost millions of lives, many more than the Americans did.

September 1st - Knowledge Day

September 1st is not really a holiday. It's the Day of Knowledge because kids go back to school on September 1st (unless it's a Sunday). We dress up even though there are no parades. My mom makes sure my school uniform is neatly pressed. She picks fresh flowers from the *klumba*, our flower garden. They are still wet with dew and I wipe the dew on my school uniform and my mom tells me to be neat and not get dirty for the big day. She puts two big bows in my hair and they slowly slide down my ponytails because they are so heavy and my hair is so thin. I adjust my bows until the First Bell ceremony is over, and after that, I put them in my *portfel* (book bag).

It is also called the Day of the First Bell because the school bell rings and school is back in session. Students return dressed up on the first day of school, and female teachers wear their best heels. Heels are a big deal in Ukraine because wearing heels makes you pretty even if it means excruciating pain, because, as we say, *"красота требует жертв,"* ("beauty requires sacrifice"). They make it through the day with some wincing but never acknowledge to each other the suffering they bring upon themselves.

Students bring bouquets of flowers for their teachers. The celebration is kicked off with an assembly in which the students line up outside the school, parents in attendance to celebrate the end of summer vacation and resumption of classes, and the bell rings to announce the first day of school. On the last day of school, usually around May 25th, there is the Day of the Last Bell, for obvious reasons. One cute tradition on that day is when a 12th grader picks up a first grade student, puts her on his shoulders, and then carries her around the sports field where all the other schoolchildren are lined up and the young first grader rings the "last bell."

Ukrainians still celebrate Knowledge Day as the first day of school. I notice that in the U.S. some holidays are connected to a day of the week and not one particular date. For example, Thanksgiving is on the fourth Thursday of the month, and Memorial Day is on the last Monday of May. In Ukraine, holidays are on particular dates.

There are no holidays between September 1st and New Year's. We definitely don't celebrate Columbus discovering America, the dead returning to haunt the living, or Pilgrims breaking bread with Indians.

There is a day for giving thanks for the harvest but is only celebrated by Protestant Christians. It's not a national holiday, but it is worth mentioning that we do take time to give thanks to God for the bountiful harvests He gives us.

Birthdays

In my family in Ukraine, birthdays are an uneventful affair with a few small gifts. No one is planning parties, mailing invitations a month in advance, buying party favors, hanging banners and piñatas, or inviting people at least three weeks in advance requesting RSVPs. Maybe that's why we don't handle the piñata well when Nicky turns three. We forget to explain to him that kids are supposed to also have a turn at hitting a piñata; it isn't just for the birthday boy to smack the heck out of it. Rob isn't much help either. He probably didn't have a piñata for his birthday either. Nicky has a fit when he realizes he has to share the bat. We take that bat away from him just in time before he starts smacking all of his guests with it. But I digress.

The celebration of birthdays in my family includes a birthday cake without candles, and maybe a gift, but I don't remember many gifts. My mom makes me a honey cake *медяник (medyanyk)*, a layered torte made with seven layers of pastry with creme, honey, and crushed walnuts in between. Birthday cakes don't come out of a box.

In terms of gifts, I only remember two from all my birthdays: a big giant bear stuffed with straw that I got for my 10th birthday, and hairspray and a Lancôme dry powder for my 16th birthday. I couldn't have been happier. I remember just barely being awake and smelling that amazing Lancôme smell. In our family, gifts are given as soon as you open your eyes: Bam! Happy birthday, Ruslana! There was no Happy Birthday song, but there were many wishes. It is common in Ukraine for your family members to stand around you and recite long poetic wishes for the birthday girl, almost like a solemn ceremony.

On my birthday, my family members line up and recite numerous wishes, saying them almost like an official proclamation, "Dear Ruslanochko, I congratulate you on your birthday! I wish you happiness, health, goodwill, and may all your dreams come true! May evil never cross your paths and only good accompany you all the years of your life!" When my parents accept Jesus in their heart, their wishes include blessings from God, wishing me to serve Him and love Him with all my heart.

Because birthday wishes are given right away in the morning as soon as you wake up, you can imagine my surprise when Rob and I were first married and I didn't get my gift first thing in the morning. I'm like, "Honey, get with the program!" He gave me some lame excuse about usually getting presents and a cake after work or school. Likely excuse.

I'll conclude this section with one of the best memories of my 10th birthday. It's February and we are gathered inside our warm house with my uncles and aunts. We eat in the *zala*, a room only reserved for guests. Our house is full of people. My dad and my uncle put me in a kitchen chair and lift me up to the ceiling and back down, saying, *"Многие лета! Многие лета!"* *("Mnogiye lyeta! Mnogiye lyeta!"* "Many years! Many years!") I am surrounded by my whole extended family, even my little brother Bogdan who is 1-year-old. I get a gigantic bear stuffed with straw. The bear is too heavy to lift, so I drag him on the ground, but he is sure huggable.

Which holidays do I celebrate in the U.S.? The American ones, for obvious reasons. I try to pull off a Ukrainian Christmas on January 7th, but everyone goes to work. I can't really celebrate Victory Day on May 9th because, in the U.S., D-Day is the big day of remembrance along with Memorial Day. While May Day, is a big holiday in the countries of the former Soviet Union, it's not a big deal in the U.S. Every May Day, Rob asks me if I am getting an itch to have a parade and roll out all my tanks and missiles and have my soldiers march in formation. I usually ignore him, but he better watch out if I ever get it in my head that I should.

CHAPTER 4

"Why Do We Need to Sit on the Luggage?"

I am 12 years old and it's springtime in Ukraine. We are visiting my *тьотя Тося*, my Aunt Tosia. My whole family has gathered together for Easter dinner. There are so many family members gathered that my aunt uses two tables to make one long one. She drapes a tablecloth over to connect both of them seamlessly. I sit down where the two tables meet. "No, no, *не сідай тут*, don't sit here." My mom is rearranging the seating to make sure I don't sit at the corner of the table. If I do, I'll never get married.

My aunt Tosia (my mom's sister) and   Uncle Yasha, August 2018.

Even though I am still a little girl, I already have many fears, most instilled through superstitions. Fear of the evil eye, fear of bad luck, fear of being insulted, fear of having a fight with my loved ones, fear of not having money, and many other phobias. The biggest fear for a girl in a village is not getting married. Now as I reflect on it, being an all-enlightened woman with a doctorate, I find these fears are downright stupid (I wonder if I'm angering some ancient pagan spirits with that statement). But … why judge my mother, my aunts, my grandmother, my neighbors, and all the female figures in my life? They, their mothers, and their mothers' mothers were all raised this way, and so it goes all the way to the pre-Christian pagan times of our ancestors who found mystical ways of explaining life events or misfortunes.

Most of the superstitions that warn me that I'll never get married are about sweeping—don't let anyone sweep around me and never sweep into the eyes of the sun (i.e., sunset).

On summer nights when I have to sweep the floor in the summer kitchen, where the door faces west, I have to hurry and sweep before the sunset. Otherwise, it has to wait to be finished in the morning. But Mom doesn't like going to bed with a dirty kitchen floor, so I have that pressure to respond to also, not just superstitions. And now, in my own household, I can't go to bed if the dishes are dirty and the kitchen is not clean. Though lately, I have found myself mellowing in this area.

The superstitions about quarreling are numerous. I guess there is a lot of fear of fighting with people.

- Don't wipe your hands on the towel together with another person. You'll have a fight with them later. (Obviously, people cared more about fighting than sharing germs.)

- Don't give something to somebody across a threshold. Don't sit on a threshold.

- Don't put keys on the table. (Honestly, people, where are you supposed to put your keys?)

- Don't spill the salt. (Salt is a significant part of our culture. Guests are greeted with salt and bread as a sign of hospitality. In Kyivan Rus, throughout the 10th to 13th centuries, salt was considered a symbol of prosperity.)

Chapter 4: "Why Do We Need to Sit on the Luggage?"

In my house and in the whole village, we believe and observe all these superstitions. My mom is the keeper of the law. I am reprimanded to not take the garbage out after sunset. "You are going to upset the evil spirits somehow." So, we have to hurry up and do it before the sun goes down or wait until morning. I. Kid. You. Not.

I wonder when I ask Rob to take out the garbage and recycling at night and he resists, is it maybe because there are evil spirits that he doesn't want to anger? I don't remember telling him that superstition though. When we were first married and were preparing to return home from Ukraine, I do remember asking him to "sit on the luggage" before the trip and he looked at me like, "Why do we need to sit on the luggage?"

Sitting on the luggage before the trip is supposed to bring you good luck on your journey. It doesn't mean you literally sit on suitcases, but rather, sitting down with your hands on your lap and being quiet for a minute and then getting up and leaving. Bible-believing Christians who still abide by these superstitions add a prayer instead of sitting there quietly to accommodate the superstition to their belief system.

Another superstition related to travel is "don't return once you've started the journey," otherwise, your journey will have misfortunes. We travel in Crimea with Julian when he is a toddler in 2004, and on the way back we forget his sippy cup at a relative's house. My dad is hesitant about returning, but he knows how important that sippy cup is for little Julian. After all, this is going to be a 14-hour drive in one day. He takes a roundabout way to avoid returning on the same road.

One superstition that totally cracks me up is "never eat from a knife." Not because it's unsafe and you can slice your tongue in half, but because if you eat from a knife, you'll become an angry person. I must have forgotten that one because I eat peanut butter and Nutella from a knife all the time.

And I'll conclude this brief chapter with the funniest superstition that always cracks me up: "If your right boob itches, someone is thinking about you." Somebody must be thinking about me right now.

CHAPTER 5

"How Did You Come to America?"

Butchering a Pig to Afford a Coat

I didn't know it at the time, but the seeds for going to America were planted in my choice of my major in college. I knew all along that I wanted to study English and with that focus in mind, I found a school that wasn't too prestigious or dependent on one's connections. In Ukraine, similar to other European countries, students choose their area of focus before entering college. I had not heard of the concept of "undecided" until I started teaching in an American liberal arts school in 2002. I knew all along that I wanted to study English to be a teacher.

I entered college in 1990 after passing three oral exams: Ukrainian language, German language, and the History of the Communist Party or the Soviet Union. To be a good teacher of English, we had to know the history of the last 70 years. Who cares about the hundreds of years of the Ukrainian history? All that mattered was seven decades of communism.

I love studying English and telling my parents about how much I learned. I finish my first year, come home in time to help harvest the potatoes in August and report to them with much excitement standing in the middle of the potato field, "Mom, Dad, the word we use in our language, basketball, makes so much sense now! It's comprised of two words, basket and ball. English is so cool! It helps me understand the words we borrowed." Thus begins my journey of expanding my mind to new ideas and new ways of seeing the world.

The year is 1992. I'm home from my second year of college. Using his architectural skills, my dad is building the first church building in the village. He'd accepted Christ in 1989, at the funeral of my grandfather who died at the age of 64 from a heart attack. Funerals of Christian believers are evangelical in nature, inviting people to accept Jesus because we never know how much we have left on this earth.

After meeting Jesus, he is told by his employer that his faith is in direct conflict with the government. He is forced out of his job and decides to follow the calling to build the first church in our village, from the ground up. The government won't let my father buy any bricks from them when they learn that they would be used for building a church. And the government owns all the businesses, so there are no alternative sources of bricks. Dad prays about it for a couple of days, relying on his faith in God, and goes back a few days later, but he is denied again. He asks more people to pray with him and after a couple more visits, the government relents. Either the prayers worked or the brick sellers tire of seeing the same guy begging for bricks. Since my dad is building the church in response to God's calling and not as his vocation, he isn't paid for his work.

With my dad building the church, there's not enough money for food and other expenses. "Let's go shopping" is a concept that doesn't exist. My roommates do not eat in a school cafeteria but bring food from home to the dorm to share. My mom packs bags full of heavy gallon-size glass jars of canned pickles, tomatoes, and salads for me to take to eat. My roommates and I take turns bringing buckwheat and other grains, along with potatoes, carrots, and beets, sharing with one another. I take the bus home once a month. The walk from the bus station to the dorm is at least a mile long, and carrying a month's supply of food, 50 pounds, causes my hands to swell and turn red, sometimes causing blisters.

In that same year when I return from college, I find myself one day in our living room in Buzhanka. Mom and Dad walk in. Mom says, "Ruslana, we have something for you. You have been working so hard in college, we bought you a gift." Mom pulls out a long cream-colored Chanel raincoat with fancy waterproof fabric and golden buttons and gives it to me. I can't believe what I see and ask with my eyes and mouth wide open, "Mom, this is so very beautiful, but how did you get the money for such an expensive coat?"

She says, "We butchered a pig and sold the meat to buy you this coat." I don't know what to say. I say "Thank you very much. Thank you. Thank you," and realize my words fail me and 10,000 thanks will not be enough. How do you thank your par-

My host mother Caryl and I. I'm wearing the Chanel coat. September 4, 1995.

ents, who spend all year raising a pig from a piglet, feeding it all year long, cleaning up after it, and then selling it so you can have a nice raincoat? It's the only item I own that's new, fashionable, and not made in the USSR. In fact, it says, "Made in Paris" on the label.

The next winter after I got my coat, my dad says, "Our American brothers and sisters in Christ sent us a package." But it's in Lysanka, five miles away. My brother and I decide to take the shortcut and go on the frozen river to Lysanka to pick up our gift. We bring the gift home and open the box with excitement. In it, there are four objects: a really nice spiral note-book for dad to write down sermons, a pair of short rubber boots for my mom, a pair of nylons for me, and a rare two-dollar bill for my brother. We are so excited about these gifts. It's like American Christmas to us! My dad solemnly says, "Let's kneel together right here, right now, and thank our generous Heavenly Father for these gifts." These two stories are not stories of poverty or how little we have. These are the stories that shaped me of what it means to be thankful for simple things.

The following summer, I meet the generous American woman Barbara Jean Alto, who handpicked these gifts for us. That summer also becomes the beginning of my story of coming to America.

Would You Like to Go to the Moon ... I Mean, to America?

There are three key figures who make America possible for me. Jesus is number one. Then my mom. Then Caryl Bloem, bless her generous heart. The reason Jesus is number one is because I meet him personally, not like face to face, but an encounter through the message of love. The year is 1992. It's right after the collapse of the Soviet Union. The newly found freedom of religion opens the door for every conceivable faith to be preached on every street corner, telling us their version of how to get to heaven. I'm happy on earth. I am not seeking any religion. The only thing I'm seeking is a guy to date.

I find a boyfriend, but his favorite "religion" is Nitzsche and Castañeda. Another guy from a local church invites me to hear John Guest, an evangelist from America, to check out the speaker's American English. We are taught British English in college, so we think American English is cool. His translator is Victor Branitskiy. (I will meet Victor later when I live in Minnesota and his wife will do my flower arrangements for our wedding. And I will later connect with John Guest and tell him my story of accepting Christ as a result of his message.)

Guest shares the message of God's love. He says, "God loves you. He gave His Son for you." I had only heard this message from my grandfather before, who was the only Christian in our family as I was growing up and was indeed persecuted for his faith. But I hear it differently this time. I pray a simple prayer asking Jesus to come into my heart. And He did. Just like that.

I head back to my dorm, walking by a woman selling flowers in the city center, the same person I have seen sitting there before, but this time I see her with new eyes. I smile at her with love. The smile is meaningful because Ukrainians don't smile just to be polite. I am overwhelmed with love. This experience is truly my own personal encounter with Jesus. I owe Him all of my life. I start attending a local church. The people welcome me with open arms but soon tell me that I need to receive the Holy Spirit to secure my salvation. They invite me into their home, I kneel, they pray over me and I receive the "tongues." I begin speaking in tongues. I have no idea what I'm saying but I know that in addition to Ukrainian, German, Russian, and English, I now have another language, but I can't interpret my own words. I'm happy to receive one more "tongue" without the long hours in the audiolingual lab. After that prayer, they tell me that I am now a legitimate Christian.

With my newly found faith and a new language under my belt, I receive an invitation to work as a translator for a group of American missionaries interpreting for street evangelism and prison ministry. During that week, my English skills skyrocket and my faith grows stronger. The missionaries I translate for are amazing people with a deep love for prisoners and common folk on the street. They don't judge me for wearing makeup and jewelry and they love my beginning level of English. I serve as their tour guide in Odessa, and when I tell them, "Follow me," they follow.

I know that they are Pentecostal Christians who came to support a local church. When I return to my home church from this mission job of translating for American missionaries, the church people don't shake my hand. They tell me that I chose to support the work of a group of disobedient Pentecostals, who were asked to leave the main congregation because they liked contemporary Christian music and clapped their hands during worship. I am utterly confused because the work these people did was transformational for local communities and prisons, but they were on some naughty list because they were clapping their hands? From this experience, I learn about the conservative, rule-following Christians who do not live by grace but by the law. I am disillusioned and disappointed in the church and quit going to church altogether, returning to my boyfriend and his "religion" of Nitzsche and Castañeda. The church members never realize that they might win the battle, but they lose the war. They definitely lost me.

Shortly before I quit that church, I come home for the summer and tell my dad that I am a Pentecostal and ask him what his faith is and if it matters. He says he is a Baptist and that he doesn't speak in tongues. He doesn't judge me for being a Pentecostal and tells me that my faith in Christ is legitimate even if speaking in tongues is confusing to me. His nonjudgmental response gives me peace about my newly found identity in Christ and I stop worrying about denominations.

"Can I still go dancing now, Dad? Can I still wear makeup?" I ask my dad nervously.

"Daughter, just listen to the Holy Spirit and He will guide you," he replies without judgment. "Not everything that's permissible is beneficial," he adds, quoting the Bible. He doesn't give me a list of do's and don'ts. Instead, he tells me that I'll know what's beneficial because the Holy Spirit that dwells within me now will guide my decisions.

The team of missionaries who came to Lysanka in 1994. Caryl is the first person on the right in the second row. The three translators are in the back. I am in the middle.

My dad tells me that American Baptist missionaries are coming to Lysanka (a neighboring town five miles away) in the summer of 1994 and that I should work as their translator. So, I agree to help out, make some money, and practice my English. I hear they pay $80 per week! That is unheard of. The American missionaries are from Minnesota and are hosting a Vacation Bible Camp for children in the community. With my previous experience as an interpreter, I am assigned as the lead translator, *perekladach,* and interpret sermons and various messages for Caryl Bloem, who is one of the most wonderful people I have ever met. I work with the American team for an entire week. At the end of the week, my mom comes to visit the camp and asks Caryl very directly if she can take me to America.

Caryl agrees to work on the invitation. I am so excited, I'm ready to quit school and just leave with them. Caryl says, "No, you need to finish your degree first." In my delirious state, I can only think, "Who needs an education when you just got invited to go to America?" I can't believe my ears that there is a possibility of me going to the United States. Growing up in a corrupt society, we didn't have posters in our bedrooms or classroom with the slogan "DREAM BIG." I couldn't dream big. I turned realist as soon as my childhood was over because the corrupt regime slaps you in the face and you wake up to the brutal reality that only people with money or connections could dream big. My family didn't have any influence in a country ridden with bribery and corruption.

Caryl turns to me and asks if I would like to come to America. It sounds like someone asking me, "Would you like to go to the moon?" No Ukrainian child from the *selo* (village) dares to dream such a dream. I do have dreams: to learn English, graduate from college, and maybe work as a translator. I love reading about international affairs, memorizing capitals of most countries in the world, and always reading the international column in the newspaper. And I would love to go to the United States. But I had been accepted into college on the condition that I'd return someday to a remote village to teach English using the "Repeat After Me" and "Read and Translate" method and couldn't dream of doing something bigger than that.

"Soviet Union: No More. Ukraine: Not Yet."

For me, my process of emigration starts in 1995, six months after Caryl returns to Minnesota. I am excited about the invitation, but first I have to get a foreign passport. All Ukrainians have a national domestic passport as their local ID, but very few people have an international passport. In 1994, Ukraine is independent, but very corrupt, with one foot still in the Soviet regime, and the other foot on a banana peel of a new wave of corruption by Ukrainian government officials. These officials are still ripping people off by passing laws for their own personal gain, and embezzlement in the government is standard practice. The government of Ukraine continues to be a kleptocracy. Government officials use government department budgets to fund their own vacations and villas. It is in this corrupt system that I go to the government office.

I show up in a government office to request a passport for traveling abroad. The worker looks at me like I was born yesterday. There is no one petitioning on my behalf, offering bribe money and expensive chocolates and liquor to grease the wheels. Imagine a nobody like me showing up in a highly corrupt office and politely asking, "Can I please have a foreign passport?" He says, "No blank booklets. Soviet Union: no more. Ukraine: not yet." What he means is that it is a time of transition from the old system to the new, down to the level of paperwork. But I know that it is his excuse to tell me, the nobody, to go home, child. No passport for you.

I bet it's hard to imagine this for those growing up in the U.S., when all you have to do is go to your local post office with an application, get your picture taken, pay a set fee, and have your passport mailed to you. I never would have gotten a passport without paying for assistance from a shady guy with an underground network who agreed to help me … for a price.

The most embarrassing part is when I ask Caryl for bribe money. I don't take time to explain to Caryl why I need money for the bribes because this is the only way of doing business in Ukraine. We are so used to it, nobody questions the practice, hence, nobody needs to explain it. It's like needing to explain why you have to go to the bathroom. That would be odd, right?

With my passport in hand, the next step is to get a U.S. visa. I receive a copy of the Minnesota senator's petition letter requesting the consul at the American embassy to grant me permission to obtain a visa to enter the U.S. I can't understand what that letter is. I had never experienced

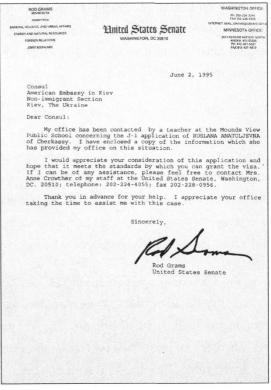

A letter to me from U.S. Senator Rod Grams petitioning on my behalf.

a government official petitioning on behalf of a nobody. Because I can't understand the power of that letter, I pay more money to gain entrance to the embassy. I later find out that the "helpful guy" with connections was practically pocketing most of the money.

It's July 1995. My father and I catch a bus to Kyiv to go to the American embassy in Kyiv to beg for a visa. Dad's car, a Zaporozhets, is not reliable enough for a four-hour trip to Kyiv. We can't afford a hotel, so we sleep overnight in a cousin's empty apartment on a couch, covering ourselves with the only thing in the room, window curtains, to keep ourselves warm. We use a couch cushion for a pillow. I am struggling to keep warm and ward off the mosquitos buzzing around my head, biting my skin.

We rise early and take a bus to the American embassy to make it in time for our 8:00 a.m. appointment. I am standing in line at the U.S. embassy with people looking at me in disbelief saying, "You are young, single, and speak English. Your visa will be denied. Don't get your hopes up." (That's an example of Ukrainian direct communication.)

This is where Jesus comes in. Jesus is working at the embassy and gives me approval for my visa. Not literally, of course. But He does the impossible. I don't have any connections with people who hold power, but I have a relationship with the One who holds all the power. Out of all of my college mates, many of whom had parents with powerful connections, no one else is getting a personal invitation to come to the U.S. I, a nobody to the corrupt but a dear child to Jesus, is the one who receives that invitation.

See, the Ukrainian government at that time is not letting anyone out of the country because young people would leave in droves. The old Soviet economy is on the brink of collapse. The free market economy doesn't exist yet. There are no jobs. The new Ukrainian currency is introduced to replace the Soviet ruble. They can't even afford decent paper to print the money on. It breaks at the crease. Plus, you need a bag of paper money to buy a loaf of bread. So, I don't blame the government for not letting a brain drain happen by letting young people leave, even if I do blame them for being corrupt and greedy and not working in the best interest of the people.

I have to pass through security just to enter into the processing office at the embassy, making my way past armed Ukrainian security forces. We stand in a long line, awaiting the moment when we have to talk to an imperious looking Ukrainian office worker tasked with receiving and rejecting requests from Ukrainian nationals to go to the U.S. The process of getting an international passport and a visa to go to America was harder than anything I've done in my life. Even my doctorate was easier. At least I was in control of the process and I didn't have to bribe my way through it.

It's my turn to go to the window to request a visa. I am motioned to a window serviced by an American office worker (versus Ukrainian). I feel relieved when I see an American smile. I learn that American workers are actually more humane. They don't treat you like an object to humiliate and exert control over. The interview goes like this.

"Why are you going to America?"
"I got an invitation from a teacher."
"What are you going to do there?"
"Teach English."

He chuckles when hearing "teach English." I couldn't have imagined that my English was good enough to teach it in American schools because my college degree was English as a Foreign Language, and I was pretty sure English was not a foreign language in the U.S. I wasn't aware that there were students in American schools who spoke English as a second language.

The office guy smiles and says, "Come back at 4 o'clock to pick up your visa." I leave the embassy skipping from joy and grinning from ear to ear telling my dad, "I got the visa! I got the visa!" All the memories of this painful process are replaced by joy and I forget my mosquito bites from the night before. My father and I lunch on apples and *kovbasa* on a bus station bench and return to the consulate at 4:00 to receive my visa. We return to the bus station to catch the next bus home.

Coming to America: Perspective of Caryl Bloem, Ruslana's American Sponsor

I asked Caryl Bloem to share the story of the work she had to do for me to get a visa and a plane ticket to America. There was a lot that happened that I was never aware of.

It was August 1995. I was sitting at my computer looking over the lake where the rain fell steadily, matching my discouragement. A team of Americans had recently returned from Ruslana's village in Ukraine where Ruslana had interpreted for them. I received a phone call from one of the team members, telling me that Ruslana was not able to get her visa. She suggested that all my striving had been in vain and it didn't look like it was God's will for her to come. I had tried everything I could think of to get Ruslana to the USA and nothing had worked. Should I give up? I wasn't sure.

A year earlier, my church, along with many other churches from Minnesota, sent a team of people to Ukraine to conduct what we call Vacation Bible School. (They called it Adventure Camp.) The Ukrainian evangelical church had experienced severe limitations and even persecution under the communist regime. They were not allowed to teach their children about the love of Jesus and had no experience working with children in the church setting. Our job was to show them how it was done and eventually train them to conduct their own camps and Sunday School programs. Of course, none of us could speak Ukrainian or Russian. Therefore, we worked through interpreters. Ruslana became my main interpreter and we quickly bonded.

At the end of the week, as we were getting ready to leave, her mother started begging me to find a way for her daughter to come to America to improve her English. Over and over, I told her it would not be possible, but she kept insisting. We had been warned that the Ukrainians might ask us to help them out in various ways, and we were not to encourage them. Evidently, any little encouragement on our part would lead them to believe we could make it happen. Try as I might, Ruslana's mother would not relent. Finally, I said I would see, but I couldn't imagine how it could happen.

After I returned to the States, I kept thinking about her request, wondering if there was any way to make this happen. I tried Bethel University, but the tuition was astronomical, and there were no scholarships available. The University of Minnesota couldn't help either, and no visa could be issued for her to work in our country. I nearly gave up. Then one day the newsletter from Education

*Minnesota mentioned an opportunity for American teachers to
participate in a program for exchange teachers. They were looking
for teachers willing to go to another country and teach while their
counterparts taught in our schools. I called the director and asked if
bringing someone from Ukraine might be of interest. He immediately
encouraged me and told me what had to be done before they could
sponsor her. We needed health insurance, life insurance that would
cover repatriation of her remains should she die here, and a letter
of support from my husband and me for food, clothing, and housing,
of course. In addition, she would need the approval of the school
district and the school principal, and round-trip airfare to come to
the USA and return to Ukraine. Quite a list!*

*Fortunately, our principal agreed and the school district superinten-
dent offered the necessary insurance, but no salary. Our school's PTA
offered to pay for her airfare. I thought we were all set. Was I ever
wrong! Even though we had all "our ducks in a row," so to speak,
the ducks in Ukraine might as well have been in Siberia.*

*The first hurdle for Ruslana became the adventure of getting an
international passport. Because the country had recently split from
the USSR, they were not prepared to issue Ukrainian passports and
they claimed not to have paperwork for any kind of passport. Months
dragged by while Ruslana chased down lead after lead. It soon
became apparent that she needed to bribe someone. As Americans,
we were appalled, but sent her money anyway. After the bribe was
offered, the official promised to get her the paperwork. She went back
time and again without success. He had taken the money with no
intention of helping her. She followed another lead, bribed another
official, and finally was able to get her passport.*

*We sent all the documentation she would need—the letter from the
Minnesota Department of Education, the letter from our school
district guaranteeing her insurance and her position, the letter from*

the PTA promising her return airfare, and the letter from my husband and me offering her a place in our home. The next step was going to the American embassy in Kyiv to get a visa.

Unfortunately, the Ukrainian guards at the embassy seemed to enjoy turning people away. Every morning people would get in line hoping for an opportunity to present their requests for visas. Hardly anyone could get past them and Ruslana was no exception. She was not al-lowed to present her papers. What else could we do? I contacted our senator, Rod Grams, and he wrote a letter supporting her. He sent a copy to the embassy but it didn't seem to do any good. She went back to Kyiv and was again turned away. By this time, it was August and school would be starting soon. What could we do?

As I contemplated our situation, the rain cleared. Shining brightly across the lake I saw a full rainbow reflected in the water. It was as if God was saying, "Don't give up. I have it all under control." When I talked to Ruslana later that week, she said she had also seen a rainbow about the same time and felt the same assurances. Shortly after that, I called the embassy in Kyiv myself and told them what we needed. This time Ruslana was able to get into the embassy and pres-ent her papers. Everything fell into place and she was able to come two weeks later. She arrived in time to begin the school year and her adventure in our country.

I think of the many ways God has used her to help so many people. I am so proud of her!

I'm thankful for all the hard work that Caryl put in to bring me here. Knowing how impossible it seemed for me to come here reminds me that it was truly a miracle for me to come to the United States.

Representing the Whole Country with Dignity

Before leaving for the U.S., I had to pack my clothes, say my goodbyes, and gather up traditional Ukrainian artifacts to bring them to Minnesota to represent my country.

> *"Mom, do we have anything Ukrainian I can bring to America?"*
> *"Everything we own is Ukrainian,"* Mom says.

But she doesn't understand. I need objects that scream "Ukrainian culture."

It's the end of August, two weeks before my departure to America. I look for cultural objects worthy of America. I look at our dishes. They look Ukrainian, but the stamp on the back reads "Gomel, Belarus," which translates as "Made in Belarus" and Belarus is not Ukraine. I consider the sunflower oil and the bread on the kitchen table. Sunflower oil is made in Ukraine, about 20 miles away from my house. That's as Ukrainian as you can get. This delicious hearty rye bread is made in Bosivka, a neighboring village, but it would never survive the trip.

My parents and my host family with the Ukrainian figurine described in this chapter.

I look around and find nothing that can be packed on the plane, carried across the Atlantic, and displayed in schools and churches where I would be presenting my cultural heritage. I keep looking and I finally find a truly Ukrainian object: a ceramic figurine of a Ukrainian man and woman lovingly embracing, dressed in traditional Ukrainian costumes.

> *"Mom, can I take this?"*
> *"Sure, that was our wedding gift. Just don't break it."*

Mom is proud that her wedding gift from 1968 is going to America to represent our homeland. I carefully take it out of the china cabinet where all the dishes are displayed. It's the only object we own that represents Ukraine in traditional ways.

But as I think about making presentations to Americans about Ukrainian culture, I realize that one figurine of a man and woman embracing is not enough to speak for our culture. Plus, I'm not sure how fifth graders are going to react to the embrace. I can hear them giggle already. I realize I need to bring more artifacts. Caryl mentioned that traditional clothing will be great to showcase. My dad runs around town asking the workers in the Palace of Culture if they can spare one costume. The Palace of Culture is our name for a community center. We are quite ostentatious with our names. But, why name something a community center when it can be a palace? And not just any palace, but a palace of CULTURE!

And to name it a community center would be a misnomer. Does your community center play Indian movies on Friday nights? Does it hold passport ceremonies when young people turn 16? As far as I know, in America, there's no ceremony when 16-year-olds get their driver's license. They are just issued a piece of paper giving them permission to drive, and a car. But there's no public ceremony with all the pomp and circumstance, celebratory music, invited guests, and a ceremonial handshake to congratulate you on turning 16 as we do in Ukraine. What would you rather have, a beautiful ceremony or a car? In Ukraine, we go for the ceremony and forgo the car because it would be far too materialistic. Or maybe it's because we can't afford a car for every 16-year-old.

So Dad and I think that maybe, just maybe, we can find Ukrainian culture in the Palace of Culture. My dad takes me with him so I can try on the costume to make sure it fits, because I will have to wear this to various schools and churches to represent my country with dignity. I am a skinny 21-year-old (this was 50 pounds ago), so the Palace of Culture worker makes sure to give me the costume with the smallest size. She understands that a piece of Buzhanka is going all the way to America.

It's an embroidered shirt and a wraparound skirt. The sleeves are so puffy, I lose my arms in them. But my fingers peek out of the cuffs. The skirt is so long it drags on the ground. The traditional Ukrainian ensemble features bright red knee-high boots with a two-inch heel, but they are too worn, she says. With a content grin on my face, I take the clothes with me, thinking that now I have a traditional embroidered costume to bring to America in addition to the figurine.

We continue thinking of where else we could search to find more arti-facts. I can't just wear the costume and stand there holding the figurine

I'm decked out in the Ukrainian costume that I brought from my Palace of Culture in Buzhanka, October 1, 1996.

in my hands. That would be embarrassing. I can already predict people asking if I can show more items from my culture. The local stores don't carry Ukrainian items because there are no tourists here and no one displays traditional objects in their houses. For example, would you be able to go to Walmart and buy a colonial costume of a Revolutionary War Minuteman or a replica of the Liberty Bell? Probably not.

Some people's houses are full of traditional objects such as embroidered pillowcases and cross-stitched *rushniky,* or table runners, to hang around the Orthodox icon on the wall. My family isn't Eastern Orthodox, hence, no icons and *rushniky* to take off the walls. Plus, it's considered old-fashioned to decorate homes with *rushniky,* and my generation is supposed to be modern and European. I don't want to have the appearance of being a peasant with our *rushniky* and other turn-of-the-century artifacts.

But my aunt doesn't care if people think she is traditional. She is Orthodox and she has icons in the corners of her house and a set of embroidered *rushniky* and pillowcases she designed herself. But they are on her pillows and I can't take those off just because I need them to represent my country in far-off America. My mom asks friends and neighbors for the *rushniky* because "*Ruslana yide v Ameriku*" (Ruslana's going to America) where she'll be representing our country. People are willing to sacrifice their lifetime supply of *rushniky* for such a noble cause. The reputation of the entire nation is at stake here.

I imagine myself standing by a table with a *rushnik* spread out and the Ukrainian figurine standing on it. I'm all decked out in my traditional costume with the puffy embroidered sleeves and I see how empty the table is where I'm representing my country. I tell my dad I need more cultural

artifacts. My dad and I get into his old Zaporozhets and drive 90 miles to Cherkassy. We had to pay $250 in bribes to the guy who was "working on my visa documents" last week, so we are left with $10 for the Ukrainian artifacts.

We go to different shops and see that the *object d'art* are too expensive for us. We end up buying two

My display of cultural artifacts representing Ukraine, October 1995.

lacquered wooden plates with the hand painted *Petrivka* floral design. The more intricate the design, the more expensive the plate. I'm looking at some plates with exquisite designs of a boy and a girl playing Ukrainian instruments in the countryside. The girl is playing the bandura and the boy is playing flute. I imagine proudly sharing with my future American audiences all about the bandura, that it has 55 strings and is more complicated than a guitar. I'm already rehearsing my future presentation, but Dad tells me we don't have enough money for the plate with the bandura. I dream about bringing a real bandura. Wouldn't that be wonderful? Dad says we can only afford plates with a simple floral pattern. We buy two, wrap them up in brown paper, and leave. On my way home, I envision standing in front of hundreds of Americans decked out in my costume, with my parents' wedding gift and the two plates spread out on the *rushniky,* and I worry about whether there is enough dignity in these artifacts for my cultural presentations. I know I should have gotten the red boots and begged the Cherkassy Palace of Culture for the bandura with 55 strings.

It's September 4, 1995. I bid a tearful goodbye to my parents and get on a plane for the first time in my life to fly to the U.S. I am 21 years old and I leave my mom, dad, my brother Bogdan, grandma, cousins, aunts and uncles, and potato fields. I am leaving my river, my hills by the river, скосогори (berms), my road that leads me to my grandma's house, the stork nest, and the school building that my

My mom and dad and brother in front of the church my dad built, 1995.

dad built. I know in my heart that I am leaving forever, not just for a year as my visa says. I know that I am not returning to the potato fields. But at the same, I have no clue what emigrating means. I don't know what the consequences are until much, much later. I am just leaving because the economy of my country is on the brink of collapse and I am young and I need a future. I am leaving to build my own future and the future of my children.

I fly through Ireland where we stop to refuel. I am on my own, wearing my Chanel coat that my parents bought for me with the money from the butchered pig. I have 20 American dollars on me, money left over from the bribe money Caryl gave me. I buy my first cappuccino and a book in English.

CHAPTER 6

"What Do You Think of America So Far?"

"Toto, I don't think we're in Buzhanka anymore."

Quoting my Japanese college exchange student who said in response to my question, "What do you think of Minnesota so far?", she said, "Yes, it's so far!". …

I sit back in the airplane seat and take a sip of the tea a flight attendant serves. I'm about to cross the Atlantic. I don't read my ticket correctly where the arrival time is listed in the local time and expect the flight to take no more than three hours. But after asking the flight attendant, I learn that I have at least eight more hours to go.

After a long flight, I arrive in Chicago, jet lagged and delirious when Caryl and her husband, Ron, pick me up at O'Hare Airport. The jet lag makes me feel like I'm on a different planet. I am disoriented but observant. The language is different, the sights and sounds are unfamiliar. Everybody speaks English around me. Even though I studied English, it sounds very foreign and I soon discover what it feels like to have a foreign language-induced headache from constant straining to make sense of what people are saying.

We drive to Caryl's aunt's house. She lives in Rockford, Illinois. The first things I notice are the shape of the house and the many rooms in it. I notice the soft carpet under my feet. In my house, we have wood floors with rugs spread out on them. I notice the color-coordinated bathroom where the floor mat and the shower curtain and the towels match. At home, we didn't bother with matching curtains and bedspreads, or even clothes, for that matter.

I don't remember what we ate for dinner, but I remember being very tired and wanting to say, "Can I go to bed?" Caryl gives me my first American words, "You may be excused." I don't understand what that means and why I need to be excused and from what. Then they say, "You can go to bed before you turn into a pumpkin." I don't understand that either and what a pumpkin has to do with anything. But I go to bed and wake up the next day, still like in a dream where I am a princess who sleeps in a soft bed with matching sheets and curtains.

I arrive in Minnesota the next day, and I am in a delirious state. We drive by hotels and residential areas and I ask, "What are those castles?" Caryl replies, "Those are people's homes. And those are hotels." My mind is struggling to process all of the differences between Ukraine and the U.S. All I see is the American wealth and the contrast of the poverty of Ukrainians compared to Americans.

The whole nation of Ukraine is poor except for the oligarchs and government officials who got rich off of embezzlement. I am conflicted about this because Ukraine is very rich in natural and human resources and yet, we are poor. I walk into an American grocery store to find it is the size of our entire school, maybe bigger. In Buzhanka, all we had was a little family store the size of a 7-11 that sold a variety of little things. I can't believe all the choices of, of all things, yogurt. All I had in Buzhanka was sour cream. Although when I bring Julian to Buzhanka in 2003, they have yogurt.

I can't believe the different kinds of ice cream in the freezer. Why do people need 31 different flavors of ice cream? All I had at home was vanilla and chocolate ice cream in sugar cones. I've never seen ice cream come in a bucket. In contrast to America, I realize that I was poor in Ukraine. It is American roads, cars, and abundance of ice cream; it is street sweepers and the ability to eat out that tells me that in Ukraine, the common folk are poor.

Ron and Caryl live in a house on the lake. I have my own bedroom with its own walk-in closet where each item of clothing is hung on a separate hanger. In my parents' house, we have a wooden wardrobe with doors where Mom and Dad hung their clothes and my clothes fit in a dresser drawer. My dad hung all his shirts on one wooden hanger and he would have to look through all of them to find the shirt he wanted to wear for work.

American walk-in closets are spacious and the number of hangers helps you see all your clothes. I hang my second-hand clothes on hangers, each piece of clothing separately. I also get a dresser with six drawers for T-shirts, underwear, sweatpants, and sweatshirts. My dresser in Buzhanka had a TV on top of it and two drawers were mine. This dresser has a beautiful mirror and I twirl around in front of it in my new second-hand clothing that Americans generously provided. I love how much new clothing I have now. I don't care that they are second-hand. I'm used to wearing second-hand clothes from my college days.

In this house on the lake, there is a bathroom right outside my door. I am happy I don't have to walk outside to use an outhouse in the winter, as I did growing up. The bathroom has matching towels, a picture of a sand dollar on the wall, and a soft rug under my feet. There is also a smaller "towel," whose entire purpose is to be used as a towel to step on when I get out of the shower. I don't know its function and I use it to dry my feet. The shower has warm running water any time of day. I thought my house in Buzhanka was pretty modern because Dad provided running water when I was in elementary school. But the water wasn't heated. In my American home, I don't have to heat the water in my bathroom by burning wood and waiting for an hour for the water to warm up.

As a little girl, I dreamt that I could just push the button and the house would be warm. My childhood consisted of heating the house in the winter by burning wood and coal in the stove. That wasn't poverty. That was the rural way of living. People in the city had gas in their apartments while rural folks had to wait until the 21st century for gas lines to be run to their

91

houses. Before natural gas, our home was heated by radiators fed with hot water running through our stove, designed by my dad.

I wonder how this house is heated and stays evenly warm and air-conditioned in the summer, 24 hours a day. I come to America and I see a button on the wall that does just that. It's a thermostat that controls the furnace to heat the house. There is no coal or wood involved. There is just a button on the wall. My dream comes true in America!

In my first month, I learn many things, such as that paper products exist for a variety of purposes. Paper towels are for wiping up spills. Napkins are for wiping your mouth when eating. Kleenex tissue is for wiping your nose. People seem to be very fluent at differentiating which paper to use for what. One day, I am homesick, standing in the middle of Caryl's kitchen crying. I cry because I was able to connect with my mom and dad by phone for the first time. This is before Skype, free international calls, and Whatsapp. Tears run down my cheeks. I sob so hard, my shoulders convulse. I reach for a napkin to dry my tears. In that emotional state, I am not thinking straight enough to decide which paper product to use. Ron hands me a Kleenex. Kleenex is softer and it doesn't rub my nose raw.

In the months that follow, I still reach for napkins to dry my tears and use Kleenex to wipe up spills because my head doesn't contain categories for paper products. When my mom visits my house and sees me use paper towels for wiping up spills, she loves that idea. When I visit my parents in 2018, I see paper towels in stores but my parents don't buy them because they are expensive and not required. They only buy them when guests come. So I buy my mom paper towels but discover they are not durable because they are made of the same material as napkins.

I'm in my host family's American kitchen. There is a dishwasher that washes your dishes and dries them! I get flashbacks to our family dinners in Ukraine and after the guests go home, women are doing dishes by hand until midnight. At my sister's wedding, we cooked for and fed 250 people.

We washed the dishes by hand. I think it took us twelve hours, if not two days. I was 14 and had the responsibility to help.

When my mom comes to America, I show her how to start the dishwasher, how to use the microwave, and how to run the washer and dryer, to which she replies, "You don't have to do housework here in America. All you do is go around the house and make sure all the buttons are pushed." She marvels that she can put her feet up and at the magic of having these inventions do all the work for her so she can get her well-deserved rest. She comments about how sparkly the dishes come out of the dishwasher. She laments that only rich people might own such miracles in their homes in Ukraine. Her heart breaks at the injustice that dishwashers, washers, and dryers are part of the standard of living in the United States, but in Ukraine, you have to be rich to deserve rest.

For Mom's 50th birthday, my brother and I buy my mom a washer. "Mom, you deserve a washer that washes and rings the clothes for you because you deserve rest," we say to her. Before this, her washer washed the clothes, but she had to wring them and rinse them by herself. My mom's hands suffered more in 50 years than anybody's hands who lived twice that long but had modern appliances helping with work.

I celebrate many Christmases in America. I am amazed at the lavish gifts children and adults get, each individually wrapped in paper. When my parents visit at Christmastime, we present our gifts to them and my dad cuts the paper with scissors to show respect to the person who wrapped it, because ripping paper is not polite. In the years that follow, I ask my mom and dad what they want as gifts to ship to them. Compared to an American's Christmas wish list, they ask for creamy peanut butter, socks without elastic, long underwear, and Ibuprofen.

I'm in an American school, and I notice a map hanging on the wall. It is not of my land but of the United States. I grew up thinking that the Soviet Union was in the center of the universe. Western Europe was on the left of the map while Asia was on the right. But the big USSR sprawled out taking over the whole map, swallowing up Ukraine and other republics in its vastness. There was no room for anything else to be visible. In the U.S.,

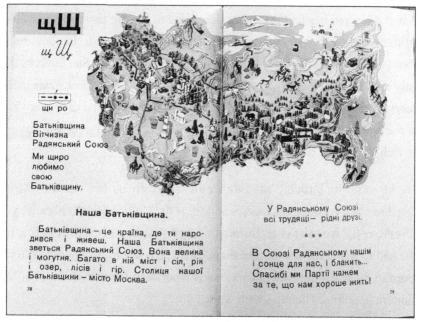

Map of the Soviet Union from our first Reader illustrating the letter shch as in the word Batkivshchyna = Fatherland. Our Fatherland is Soviet Union, we proudly said.

when I notice the map featuring the United States in the middle, my center is displaced, both on the map and internally. I don't see the Soviet empire on the map. I don't see myself on the map. I know that I'm no longer home.

Over the next weeks and months, I am exposed to so many new events, items, people, cultural norms, and thoughts that I can't possibly remember them all. It's like Dorothy when she went over the rainbow. She struggled to understand everything going on around her, but like Dorothy, I just keep putting one foot in front of the other, following the yellow brick road.

In the years to come, I start noticing deeper things, not just the obvious differences such as food, flags, and festivals, but the deeper cultural nuances. In the process, I become an amateur anthropologist as Eva Hoffman aptly points out in her interview:

> "...every immigrant becomes a kind of amateur anthropologist —you do notice things about the culture or the world that you come into that people who grow up in it, who are very embedded in it, simply don't notice. I think we all know it from going to a foreign place. And at first you notice the surface things, the surface differences. And gradually you start noticing the deeper differences. And very gradually you start with understanding the inner life of the culture, the life of those both large and very intimate values. It was a surprisingly long process is what I can say."

One of the first deeper cultural nuances I learn about America is American philanthropy. Regular folks have money (not just rich oligarchs like in Ukraine), and Americans are generous with their money. In the first year of our marriage, Rob's family and friends help me raise funds for my dad to buy a tractor to help him cultivate his fields. Later, my colleagues and friends donate toward my friend's cancer treatment, expecting nothing in return. One person gives almost $600 saying "I'm just paying it forward because of the kindness I've been shown as an immigrant when I arrived." Facebook friends whom I only know from social media but have never met face-to-face, give donations to help my dad install new windows in the church where the elderly had to wear coats because of the draft coming from the old windows. They give funds towards my dad's van for his church. I am amazed and deeply thankful. I am in a coffee shop and they tell me, "This latte is free. It was provided to you by a local senior center. Here's a brochure if you want to know more." They are not even asking for donations. They just freely give because they have freely received.

My friend Luda tells me that this is in stark contrast to Ukraine where such acts of kindness are not frequent, and if somebody gives you something for free, it's considered suspicious activity. I love philanthropic America, the America that gives with no strings attached.

CHAPTER 7

"Why Do Ukrainians Share Towels?"

The Holodomor: Russia's Starvation of the Ukrainian Nation

As a freshly minted immigrant moving to America, I quickly find that many Americans are very independent, preferring to work for themselves, to be socially and financially independent, relying on no one but themselves, and owning their own things. I'm told that the American dream is to own your own car and house, to have a family, and to maintain that same pioneer spirit that drove early settlers westward.

Of course, Ukrainians wouldn't mind owning their own car and a house, if they could only afford it. But in general, Ukrainians are much more codependent and collective-minded. I try to understand the causes of these collectivist tendencies among Ukrainians with some confusion, because I know that historically Ukrainians have been fiercely independent, fought for their own country, and wanted to own their own land.

In 1919, when Ukraine stopped being Ukraine and became a Ukrainian Soviet Socialist Republic, Soviet authorities systematically eliminated Ukrainian national and ethnic identity, language, and family traditions as they fostered socialist, collective identity. Not only ideologically, but also materially. The private farms of many Ukrainians were taken by force during the "collectivization" era. Those who opposed collectivization were labeled with a derogatory term, "kulak," which means a fist. The tightly clenched fist symbolized people firmly hanging on to their land.

Then the period of *roskulachennia* (getting rid of the kulaks) started. Those efforts led to the artificial famine of 1933 ordered by Stalin during which an estimated three to six million Ukrainians were starved to death. This is referred to as the Holodomor, an event orchestrated by Stalin by depriving Ukrainians of any access to food. Many recognize it as genocide, an ethnic cleansing that punished independently minded farmers for their desire to own their own land. In those times, one could be independent and dead, or collectivized and alive. Many Ukrainians would rather fight for their freedom than give in to the tyranny of a foreign oppressor, a notion familiar to Americans. But in the Holodomor, the opposing force was too great and millions of Ukrainians were starved to death.

"Why Can't You Just Borrow an Axe from a Neighbor?"

"Ru, I need to go to Home Depot. I need to buy an axe."

"Honey, just borrow an axe from a neighbor," I advise my husband.

"Oh shoot, I need a tablespoon of cinnamon and I'm completely out," I say, making my first-ever pumpkin pie.

Rob replies jokingly, *"Just run across the street and borrow it from our neighbor."*

He replies jokingly because it's something you don't do in the Midwest. Of course, it depends on the relationship you have with your neighbors whether or not you'll run over to borrow an egg or a cup of sugar or an axe. My current neighborhood is very friendly, and I could run over to the neighbor and borrow whatever I needed. My neighbors are kind, generous, and they are more than happy to let me borrow an axe, and even offer a splitter, and anything else I might find useful in their garage. But I find it's not a common practice here, so I develop my self-reliance and am thankful for a small grocery store in town just a bike ride away.

My dad has flown here to spend time with us in the U.S., and he is helping me with splitting elm wood. Elm trees are known for their tightly interwoven fibers. They are nearly impossible to split by hand. Most people use a hydraulic splitter. My dad splits a 50-year-old elm with a wedge that we borrow from my neighbor. I am amazed at his strength. When the job is done after a few days, he says to me, "Let's return these tools right away. I never borrow anything. I prefer to own my tools." I realize that my notion of borrowing and lending are based on only my assumptions and limited experiences in the '80s. Borrowing an egg or a tablespoon of sugar is okay, but a man must own his own tools!

To Conform or Not to Conform?

During Soviet times, people are expected to conform to society's expectations, and the Soviet regime imposes a collectivist mentality on its people. It's not really a mentality of people watching out for one another, but more that we are one homogeneous mass of Soviet people blindly following Communist Party propaganda. We aren't encouraged to be proud of Ukraine as a nation or Ukrainians as a distinct people, let alone being proud of being unique individuals. If you want to be unique or disobey the Party's orders, your destiny includes being rejected by society or sent to the gulags. Very few individuals are strong enough to withstand that kind of pressure.

In educational settings in the '80s, individual viewpoints are never solicited. It is expected for everyone to conform to society's opinion. I don't remember a single occurrence of any teacher asking me, "What is your opinion, Ruslana?" I am taught to think what everyone else thinks, and not to think for myself. In the U.S., it takes some rewiring to formulate my own opinions. But the other extreme exists in the U.S. and Ukraine as well: too many opinionated people expressing their beliefs with no factual basis to support their opinion.

Working together as a team is a common approach for getting things done in Ukraine. Also, offering assistance and accepting help is more common in Ukraine than what I've experienced in Minnesota. I have a tendency to offer my help to people and most times people reject my offer of assistance politely. In response, I often hear, "Thanks, I'm fine," "Thanks, I got this." There is this pervasive attitude of self-reliance that is held as a core value of what it means to be an American.

It's my first year as an exchange teacher in an American school. I notice contrasts with what I grew up with in the '80s and early '90s in Ukraine. Individual creativity and exploration of ideas through art is highly encouraged, even though students aren't producing masterpieces. In Ukrainian art classes, my drawings were judged according to how well I copied the example provided by my teacher. The lines had to be straight, drawn with a ruler, and we weren't allowed to draw outside the lines. Finger painting didn't exist even in preschool. My mom didn't put my creative art on the refrigerator because it wasn't perfect and because it was considered bragging.

I am in my late 30s in Minnesota and I finally begin discovering myself as an individual, distinct from society. I do have America to thank for that. I pursue a doctorate in my 40s and write this book. I feel free to be myself even in little things, like what I wear when going out in public. I don't always have to be dressed up when going out in public. Rob reminds me that I used to dress up just to go to the grocery store. But about 10 years into it, I feel the freedom of going to the grocery store wearing my sweatpants and a baseball cap. It takes me years to get there, but once I do, it is fabulous. Parents in the U.S. don't judge me for how I dress my children either. If anyone judges me, it is their problem. It is in these aspects that America is the land of the free for me. I'm no longer a slave to the public image. If I dress up, I do so for myself.

"You are special." (Mr. Rogers)

I am in fourth grade. The year is 1984. Ukrainian kids, like most kids on the planet, enjoy bragging about themselves, thinking that the universe revolves around them. As a 9-year-old, I say, "I have four apples and you only have two!" My friends say, "Teacher, I already solved this math problem!"

The teachers rarely say, "Good job." Instead, they respond to our bragging with, "*Я остання буква в алфавіті,*" which translates into, "I is the last letter in the alphabet." The letter *Я*, which is pronounced Ya, means I, as in "I am so awesome." If you look at the Ukrainian alphabet you'll notice that the backwards R, *Я* (Ya), is the last letter in the Ukrainian alphabet. It is our teacher's way of teaching us some humility and to not start every conversation with "*Я, Я, Я*" ... "Me, Me, Me."

I'm in my first year of teaching in Minnesota, and I see kids read the book *I Like Me* by Nancy Carlson. The title surprises me. Now, I see value in having healthy self-esteem and liking yourself. The Ukrainian people tend to view themselves on the whole as having low self-esteem. As a result of being seen as second-class citizens by the ruling Russians during the Soviet era, Ukrainians developed a national inferiority complex. But since Ukraine's independence in 1991, there has been a resurgence of pride due to the re-establishment of the Ukrainian national identity.

During my school years, personal and individual identity is not talked about. The concept and the word emerge later, when Ukraine begins to rebuild after becoming independent again. By that time, I am in the United States. And I discover that in the United States, I can redefine my identity. I take on many identities and they expand throughout my life. I am no longer defined by only my national identity. I discover that I am an extrovert. I take personality tests like Myers-Briggs and StrengthsFinder and discover new categories to define myself. I am also a mom, a wife, a Christ-follower, a friend, a daughter, an academic, a linguist. I engage in identity exploration as I take on new roles. I don't question or have to negotiate any of those identities, except for one—my new identity of being an immigrant.

CHAPTER 8

"Mom, Why Do You Say it That Way?"

Learning English With the Audiolingual Method

"Down, town. Downtown bus.
"Down, town. Downtown bus."
"Engine, engine number nine. Going down Chicago line."

I t's 1992, the second semester of college. It's a typical Wednesday evening, 7 p.m. I am in an audiolingual lab chanting meaningless rhymes to practice the diphthong "ow" as in down and town. The lab consists of individual booths with desks and dividers, a tape player, and headphones. I am studying English at the Cherkassy Bohdan Khmelnytsky Pedagogical University. If you can pronounce that, you can be an honorary member of the Cossack community and wield a булава (*bulava* or mace).

The pronunciation drills are as dull as a blade on a neglected scythe. Pronunciation drills serve their own purpose, I deduce. Twenty-five years from now, my enlightened self, with decades of educational linguistic theory and experience under her belt, will have shivers sent down her spine when reflecting on the methodology our professors used to teach us English in the 1990s.

It is called the audiolingual method. The idea behind this innovative pedagogy is that we learn by listening and repeating. Reminds me of "rinse and repeat." Some professors argue for its value and being immersed in the sounds, but I wonder why meaning has to be sacrificed. We spend two hours three times a week for at least three years in a row in the sound lab with headphones on chanting jump rope rhymes or choosing rhymes like "Engine, engine number nine. Going down Chicago line."

Now as I write this, Rob asks me if in addition to Engine, Engine, Number Nine if we learned Bubble Gum, Bubble Gum in a Dish. It goes like this:

> *Bubble gum, bubble gum in a dish*
> *How many pieces do you wish?*
> *Four!*
> *One, two, three, four,*
> *And that means you are not it!*

I can't imagine having a rhyme about bubble gum when I was growing up because the Soviet gum I chewed never made any bubbles. Soviet bubble gum quickly lost its sweetness, so I got in the habit of dipping it in sugar over and over again. (When I moved to the U.S., I think I personally financed my dentist's annual trips to the Bahamas on my cavities alone.)

Our choosing rhymes weren't as sweet. The ones we recited caused nightmares in children. Here's one of those rhymes. To keep the original meaning of it, I couldn't translate it accurately and rhyme it at the same time. So, I went for meaning.

> *The moon came out of the fog*
> *The moon took the knife out of its pocket and said*
> *I'll cut you, I'll beat you*
> *Who will be your friend?*

That's the short version. The longer version includes a line about stabbing your daughter to death. This pretty much sums up how sweet my childhood was.

Our English learning also includes learning traditional songs. One of my favorites is, "Oh, Shenandoah, I long to hear you." The copy of our text is so worn out that the line on the last *h* is erased, making it look like an *n*, and we all sing, "Oh, Shenandon," not Shenandoah. Nobody corrects us or explains what or who "Shenandon" is (this was before Google). Believe me, I know learning pronunciation has its place because the sound system of both languages and the intonation patterns are indeed different. I also believe that those goals can be achieved more meaningfully.

In these audiolingual phonetics classes, teachers are more interested in teaching us how to pronounce Jaguar and Shenandon than taking the time to teach us the cultural knowledge of the English-speaking countries. After the song Shenandoah, my second favorite is, "Oh Susanna, oh don't you cry for me, I've come from Alabama, with a banjo on my knee." But no one takes time to explain what Shenandon is or who Susanna is and where the heck Alabama is.

I am not sure if we sing the original lyrics or a revised version. The original lyrics, I learn when researching for this book, were brutally racist, but most Americans aren't aware of that. Even husband Rob told me they were singing the song in first grade! The opportunity to learn about the racist origins of that song is lost because the teachers aren't aware of those origins. And why am I even singing about Alabama when I was sitting in an audiolingual booth in the middle of Ukraine, in Cherkassy, a city not on the river Shenandoah but the Dnieper?

Don't even get me started on the banjo. Have you heard of learning languages using pictures? Not in my day! We never get to see a picture of a banjo, and the closest thing my mind could visualize is a bandura because it also starts with a b. Plus, bandura is a Ukrainian musical instrument, something I know. A banjo was, well … it might as well have been a three-legged alien and I wouldn't know why it's "on my knee" causing Susanna to cry in Alabama.

Because I am majoring in English, we also read dozens of American novels. I enjoy reading literature more than our pronunciation lessons in the lab. The literature we read has profound meaning. Although I can't understand every word, I can understand bigger themes of love, hope, and sacrifice.

We read Ray Bradbury's *Fahrenheit 451*. Too much culture is packed into those novels, and without a historical and cultural background, it's hard to understand what's in front of me on those pages. We discuss the ideas behind book burning but, ironically, we are not making connections to the gulags and how anti-communist ideas were banished, similar to book burning.

I learn the word mortgage from *Sister Carrie* by Theodore Dreiser, but I can't connect any meaning to the word because there is no such concept in my culture. Nobody takes out a loan to buy a house where I live. In the cities, people buy an apartment. In the country, my parents own their own home that they built themselves without taking out any loans. We read *Catcher in the Rye* and have deep discussions about the innocence of childhood and all I think about is the work I was forced to do from third grade up in the potato fields along with the grown-ups. We read *A Prayer for Owen Meany* by John Irving, and I am proud to say that it becomes one of Rob's favorite books (and Rob is a literature buff).

I realize that my favorite book by far is a collection of short stories by O'Henry. I sob when reading the story *The Last Leaf,* which is about a woman dying of pneumonia. She decides to hang on to life until the last leaf is blown away from the branch outside her window, but someone paints the shadow of the leaf on her bedroom wall to resemble a real tree, and so her hope never dies. In another short story by O'Henry, I love reading about two people madly in love with each other and how they each sacrifice their most treasured possession to buy a Christmas gift for the other, and that's how I discover *The Gift of the Magi*. I come to America and tell everyone about my discovery of a collection of short stories by O'Henry, and not many people share my enthusiasm except for Rob because he loves good literature.

At the age of 21, during the American literature classes, I discover American children's literature by reading Anne of Green Gables and Wizard of Oz. I fall in love with the characters and their adventures. They take me into new cultures, teach me about Midwestern natural disasters (such as the tornado), and describe places like Kansas that I've never heard of before. I'm like Dorothy. My geographical, cultural, and linguistic worlds expand, even if it's only in the pages of books. I do not even dare to imagine that one day these worlds will be completely transformed when I emigrate. For now, I'm satisfied with my imaginative travel through various story worlds.

Our instructors follow the methodology of the more formal the better, and we are taught to speak English in a bookish way. We learn how to say moreover and furthermore to connect our ideas in speaking. No one teaches that those connectives are only for academic writing or conference presentations. We sound like robots who can't adapt their language to context of the situation or culture.

We are taught British English, using books and materials from Great Britain, and learn their values at the same time saying things like, "May I borrow your Jaguar?" I learn to say biscuit for cookie, lorry for truck, lift for elevator, so I am amused when people in Minnesota say chocolate chip cookies and refer to doggie treats as biscuits. I pronounce fragile and futile in British ways. I quickly switch over to American English when it comes to vocabulary and pronunciation, but spelling takes longer. Some Americans, who don't know that the origin of my misspellings are from my training in British English, tell me my spelling of analyse, organise, dialogue, and catalogue are wrong. I feel invalidated in those corrections because I have always thought of myself as a pretty strong speller. I don't have an understanding of language use yet to tell myself that language is not right or wrong, but that rightness and wrongness are determined by the context of culture and the context of situation. That awareness comes later.

So, it is with this knowledge of classic American literature, how to say, "May I Borrow Your Jaguar?" "Engine Engine Number Nine," and "Banjo on My Knee in Alabama," that I come fully prepared to speak English when I finally arrive in Coon Rapids, Minnesota, on September 4, 1995. No one is holding a banjo on their knee in Minnesota, and no one is driving a Jaguar around. All I see are Chevys, Pontiacs, and Ford trucks with big wheels. There is no Shenandoah, but I do find a "Land of 10,000 Lakes" proudly etched into every license plate.

Pronunciation as a Source of Laughter and Embarrassment

Rob has a friend whose name is Doug. The /o/ in Doug is the same sound as /o/ in dog to me. Most of my conversations about going to Doug's house end up like this and now have become an inside joke.

> Julian: *"Where are we going?"*
> Me: *"We are going to Dog's house."*
> Julian: *"What's the dog's name, mom?"*
> *"Dog's dog's name is Abby,"* I reply.

The vowels are a real pain in the behind. In year one of phonetics class, I am holding my hand under my chin and learning how to pronounce *a* as in bag, opening my mouth wide, making sure my chin touches my hand held beneath it. It is physically exhausting to try to open my mouth so wide (vertically wide, not grinning from ear to ear) to make that sound. I'm thinking, "How can people speak this language? Your face hurts from it!" I don't have all the muscles developed for those sounds. In Ukrainian, there is only one "eh" sound, there is no need to confuse foreigners by pronouncing it in four different ways (like in bed, bad, edge, apple, etc.) or not saying it at all as in silent *e* as in crane or pine.

Knowing how to properly say "ay" by holding the back of my hand to my chin, I come to a state where they say bag in a Minnesotan way, bayg. You have to stop just before it becomes an "ay." So all my work to ensure my chin touches my hand are useless here because no one says bag the way we were taught in the audio lab. But as a native speaker, you never have to ponder such things as how you say bag differently from how the International Phonetic Alphabet lists it /æ/ as in hand, flap, had, and mad.

You are probably thinking, "It must be so hard for non-native speakers to pronounce English. I had no idea we said things that way." It depends on whose English it is: the frozen-in-time audiolingual lab English that only stays in the lab (because no one talks like the people on those cassette tapes) or the English that real people speak. I am sharing these challenges to help native speakers see what it is like to learn your language from a non-native speaker's perspective. When I teach Ukrainian, I am able to look at my native language from the outsider's point of view because I already went through that process when learning English.

The picture below illustrates the serious business of learning English as a lifelong journey in a humorous way. As you can see, I'm about halfway through my journey.

I love the journey, including those instances as illustrated below. Sometimes they are a source of laughter for everyone involved.

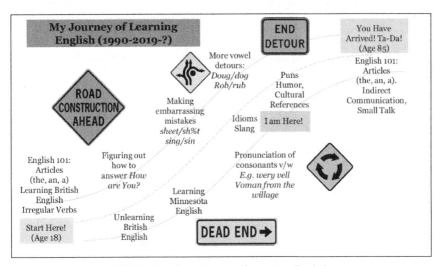

My Never-ending Journey of Learning English.

I'm on the phone with a principal interviewing him about the methodology for meeting English learners' needs for my class assignment.

> *"What kinds of activities do teachers often do to help ELLs [English language learners] understand what they read?"* I ask.

> *"Definitions of vocabulary words and comprehension questions,"* he replies.

> *"How about workshits?"*

> *"Oops, I mean worksheets. I'm sorry, it's an ELL thing,"* I say, trying to recover.

And I wasn't even swearing, even though I wanted to, because as one educator said, "Worksheets don't grow dendrites." So, maybe it wasn't a pronunciation issue, but a Freudian slip?

Another pronunciation slip happens when I am wearing the traditional costume that I borrowed from the Palace of Culture in Buzhanka during a presentation at church. Someone asks, "When do you wear this outfit?" I reply with, "We wear them when sinning (instead of singing)." In other words, we wore business casual for all our righteous acts and the traditional outfits were used for sinning.

How to Speak Minnesotan

> *"So, where did you learn how to speak English so good?"*

> *"I studied English at the Cherkassy University named after Bohdan Khmelnitsky for five years. Moreover, I practiced my English when translating for missionaries. Furthermore, I read several volumes of American literature at my university."*

> *"Wow, your English is impeccable."*

Impeccable, for sure. Robotic is a more apt description. I sound very formulaic and memorized, like speaking from a dictionary. In all my five years of studying at the university, I have one or two interactions with a native English speaker visiting our university, and his job is to teach us colloquial English. He sits in the chair and we gather around him, sitting in a circle listening to him like he is from another planet. He doesn't use furthermore and moreover, his language is kind of sloppy, talking the way regular people speak as they go about their day.

His job is to teach us slang. He says, "quit pulling my leg," "awesome," "hang out," "yep," and "yeah." We are mesmerized. We never encountered words like these in the literature we read. We are taught to say splendid rather than awesome, "don't lie to me" for "you're pulling my leg," "visit with each other" versus "hang out," and "yes, indeed" and never "yeah" and "yep." We listen to and marvel at the American speaker, and in our appreciation, we say, "You have saved our lives. We are eternally grateful," like the aliens from *Toy Story*. After a 30-minute interaction with him, we go back to our grammar translation exercises and audiolingual booth where we say "yes, indeed," and "splendid."

In Minnesota, I learn that people are sloppy with their language. They say "anyhoo" instead of "moreover." I wonder if they had any formal education in the English language. But I know that there is something wrong with my furthermores and moreovers because I get funny looks and facial expressions that say, "You sound different." In their defense, it is a natural reaction to something "not quite from here," not quite what they are used to. It is English, but it is a different kind of English, different in sound and different from "Minnesota Nice" because I sound too direct, I don't understand indirect communication, and I say "yes, indeed," and "splendid." But I quickly catch on to "yeah" and "awesome."

I also quickly discover that people don't speak British English or even Standard American English in Minnesota. In the Great White North, everyone thinks they speak Standard American English, but they don't. They speak Minnesotan English. My host mom gives me the book *How To Talk Minnesotan* by Howard Mohr when I arrive. I feel very confused when she hands it to me. I thought my days of studying English from books were over when I graduated from college with a degree in English. Looking at that book, I was like, "Wait, Minnesotan is a language?"

I honestly can't understand anything in the book and believe me it isn't written in Chinese, it is in English. There are pages with rules about maintaining one's personal distance, not speaking too loudly, not saying things directly because it would offend people, and ways of saying hello and goodbye.

In my daily communication, I often hear the phrase, "That's different," which takes me a long time to understand and use. Borrowing from Dr. Seuss, it really makes my puzzler hurt from puzzling over it so much. Different from what? What do you really mean when you say, "That's different"? Do you mean it's different from what I expected it be? Do you mean, it's different than the last hot dish you made? Do you mean you don't like it?

Or when they don't want to hurt your feelings and don't want to say that they don't like your green bean casserole or hot dish because you put curry in it (a flavor unknown to most Minnesota hot dishes), they say, "That's different." The most typical meaning associated with that phrase is "I don't like it," or "It's weird." But people don't even say, "I don't like it." Instead, it's "I don't care for it or I could care less." Basically, whenever you hear "that's different," there is a negative meaning behind it.

I am at Purple Goose, a store in Verona that specializes in unique outfits. I am looking around and find a blouse that is indeed different from anything I own. I take it off the rack and say, "That's different!" (as in unique). I see the reaction of the salesperson and instantly realize that what I said was exactly what I meant, but how it was interpreted by the salesperson was, "That's weird." I quickly corrected myself and said, "I love this. This is so unique, and would really spice up my wardrobe."

I learn how people in the Midwest exchange thank yous. It's quite funny, actually. It goes like this,

"Thank you so much for doing that."

"No, thank YOU."

"Oh no, no, thank you."

"No, really, thank YOU."

And it goes on and on for a while until someone finally says, *"You are welcome."*

Over time, colloquial English grows on me. I have a pretty strong command of the straightforward language but idiomatic language takes longer. I say phrases like, "We can't let the tail wag the dog," "Don't make mom fly off the handle" (that one comes in very useful!), "Let's go hang out," "Let's go to a burger joint," and many others. I use these phrases to "acquire America" and make it my own, as if it belongs to me too, just the same way it belongs to those who say those phrases effortlessly without thinking twice or butchering them. My husband tells me that "let's go to a burger joint" isn't something people say now unless it is meant ironically. It's a thing of the past. I realize that my efforts to make America my own will have to be done using other resources because it ain't workin' with colloquial idiomatic language.

Most cultural references are also lost on me. I don't understand when people refer to movie references, songs, and historical events before 1995. Rob shows me dozens of movies and documentaries like *Twelve Years a Slave, Amistad, All the President's Men (Watergate), the Vietnam War, the Civil War, Bury My Heart at Wounded Knee*. I also watch classics with him like the *Wizard of Oz, Gone with the Wind, Citizen Kane, A Streetcar Named Desire*, and many more. In this process, I learn to understand cultural references like, "If I only had a brain," and many others.

Personal Space in Public Midwestern Spaces

I am in my first year as an exchange teacher, supposedly teaching, but learning more about the American culture of the Midwest. I have to get through a gaggle of kids sitting on the carpet. I know you use the word gaggle to refer to geese, but don't you think "gaggle of kids" is just the perfect way to describe them? Just imagine 20 kids sitting on the carpet and you'll get the picture.

So, I am trying to squeeze by the kids to get to the front of the room, to teach another Ukrainian culture lesson. The kids aren't aware, and neither am I, that figuring out how to get through the group of kids sitting on the floor is indeed teaching and learning a cultural lesson. But that's what I meant when I said at the beginning of the book that you have to live long enough in both worlds to see the differences and categorize those as cultural norms. As I am shuffling my feet to work my way through the group, the kids don't move. I say, "Let me through," and the kids look at me funny. I am speaking English, aren't I? But I realize I need to say, "Excuse me."

I observe how people walk in public places like grocery stores and museums and see that even if you don't bump into another person, but are only three feet away, you say "I'm sorry" or "Excuse me." I am baffled because "Sorry" and "Excuse me" are thrown around mindlessly. I don't understand why they are constantly apologizing. In Ukraine, we use those words to apologize for an offense. I am in constant conflict with myself and my new culture and this new language, learning how to be polite, and learning which definition of politeness to be guided by. I wonder what offense was carried out when I hear people walk by each other and say, "Excuse me."

I share my confusion and my friend Sharon enlightens me with, "We say excuse me to announce that we are about to invade someone's personal space." All of the confusion is clarified for me now. I realize that notions of personal space guide this cultural behavior and their linguistic realizations. I learn again that translating across languages is more than translating words, it is indeed a process of translating across cultures. However, I am fully aware that understanding the reasoning is helpful, but being fluent in that practice is a whole other thing. "Translation" is never finished as I continue to negotiate my way through these cultural practices because they extend beyond language.

You see, in Ukraine, people aren't as particular about having their personal space invaded. People learn how to slither their way through the crowds without being noticed. People are more comfortable with bumping into each other without having to excuse themselves. The Global Security blog (www.globalsecurity.org) provides an accurate foreigner's insight of personal space in Ukraine:

> *"The invasion of personal space seizes the attention of many foreigners. First, there is the practice of standing close in lines or standing a bit too close when speaking to you. Cutting in lines and even shoving in crowds, while never personal, is common. Moreover, no one would ever apologize for this. (If you happen to, they'll know right away that you are foreign, but they probably already know.)"*

In Ukraine, when you walk through a crowd, you don't say "Excuse me." You rarely say anything. You just move and people get out of the way. If you have to say something because you are in a rush and people don't move out, you say, "Let me through, *bood laska* (please)." The tone of voice communicates the implied "please." Sometimes, you have to throw an elbow or two at busy bus stations or bus stops and for peak hours.

But what I learned in Ukraine in my English classes was that "Excuse me" is only for these instances: "Excuse me, what time is it?" or "Excuse me, where is the metro?" When I am in Minnesota (and most public spaces in the U.S.), I learn that I need to expand my use of "Excuse me" to announce that I am about to encroach or invade someone's personal space. It doesn't bother me if someone grabs something off the shelf in the grocery store and they reach in front of me without saying "Excuse me." In Ukraine, we want to be the least intrusive we can, so we just grab an item off the shelf and quickly disappear. No need to draw attention to yourself with an "Excuse me."

My son Nicky and I are in a grocery store in the winter of 2019. We are navigating a very busy, pre-apocalyptic looking store where people are grabbing food and water like there was an impending alien invasion. I am pushing my cart gently through the aisles and have to make a tight turn and say, "Let me through," in a very polite voice, sometimes saying "please," sometimes just using my non-verbals to communicate the implied "please." The guy looks at me like I stabbed him in the kidney or stepped on his toe. His face says, "That's the rudest thing I've heard all day. What's wrong with that woman?" Nicky looks at me and gently says, "Mom, why did you say it that way? We say, 'Excuse me.' We don't say 'Let me through.'" I feel so embarrassed, I almost fall through the floor. (Rob has informed me that "falling through the floor" must be a direct translation from Ukrainian because in the U.S. that phrase is reserved for talking about the stock market crashing). Here I am, having lived in this country of my dreams for 24 amazing years, speaking this language for 24 years (plus five years of studying it in the audiolingual lab) and I still resort to my own way of speaking by directly translating word for word the Ukrainian phrase *Пропустіть, будь ласка* (Let me through, please).

Ironically, when I go back to Ukraine, the reverse happens. I resort to the ways I learned in the U.S. to get through crowds. One day, I am with my dad in the grocery store. We are almost at the checkout register. I realize that I forgot to get a particular kind of candy for my boys to bring back as a gift. So, as I am walking through the line of people, I politely say, "Excuse me," in Ukrainian. Ukrainians look at me funny and one guy says, "What are you apologizing for?" My behavior is very odd to the Ukrainians. Sometimes I don't feel like a spoon or a fork. What does that make me, a dork?

I forget how to be Ukrainian when I'm in Ukraine, and I'm not quite American when I'm in America. In America, I am Ukrainian-American, but when I'm in Ukraine, I'm an Americanized-Ukrainian, *американезована українка*. Where do hyphenated people belong? I feel like I'm too American to be Ukrainian, but I'm too Ukrainian to be American. Like a spork, I don't have my own place in the drawer.

I feel fortunate that I have grown to have the frame of mind to be able to mull over my place in this world. Were I preoccupied about food, shelter, and employment, I wouldn't have the presence of mind to be able to wrestle with my immigrant identity crisis. As I rise through the plateaus of Maslow's Hierarchy of Needs, I find myself worrying less about shelter, food, and clothing, and focus more on personal development, career, and my developing immigrant identity. Immigrants who always live in survival mode may not have the brain space to think about their cross-cultural identity. They worry about putting a meal on the table or paying bills or their aging parents an ocean away.

I continue to search for what it means to be American. I read books by other immigrants who tell introspective stories about their cross-cultural journeys. I have conversations with my husband about my identity crisis and he always listens and talks me off the ledge. I have supportive co-workers who study identity and who understand me and can finish my sentences. I find myself in good company with other people who live between two worlds or people who have lived abroad and can analyze cross-cultural nuances of their own culture. When I talk with them, it helps me understand myself and others better.

CHAPTER 9

"Hi. How Are You? How Was Your Weekend?"

When "How Are You?" Doesn't Mean How Are You?

"Hi, how are you?"

"Well, since you asked, my dog has diabetes and I was up three times with him, so I feel pretty crummy and tired. I spent all morning cleaning up the pee where he sleeps, spilled my coffee, and just had one of those mornings. You know?"

With my friends, I can actually have a conversation like that, but for the most part, "How are you?" is just a casual greeting and no one has the time or cares enough to listen to your entire life story.

In the Midwest, particularly in Minnesota and Wisconsin, the communication patterns that make me feel "not from here" are greetings, engaging in small talk, and interpreting indirect communication. To understand my learning journey of those aspects of communication in the Midwest, it will help if I explain how those communication practices are carried out in Ukraine. In Ukraine, "How are you?" is not a greeting. Small talk is considered being fake, and indirect communication means you are not being honest.

In terms of "How are you?" the only context where that question is used is when people have a close relationship, such as friends or family, and are interested and ready to hear all the details about someone's life. In other words, Ukrainians don't ask "How are you?" as a greeting. When they greet you, they generally ask you specific questions. The type of question depends on the context of situation, such as your relationship with people, the time of year, whether it's an urban or rural setting, and other variables. One summer when I was visiting my dad, I heard people ask each other, "How is your goat? Does your goat give a lot of milk this year? Are the chickens laying eggs?"

It's Sunday morning. My dad is on his way to the church where he is a pastor. His job is to pick up the elderly churchgoers in his van. Elderly people in rural Ukraine do not own their own cars or go on vacations. They are poor, their pensions are barely enough to cover the electricity bill, let alone go on vacations. Many of them suffer from severe osteoporosis. They rely on canes to get around, and there's no morning bus to get them to church. They rely on my dad to pick them up and give them a ride, which my dad does gladly.

As these *babusias* (grandmas) are getting in the car, the first question my dad asks after saying *Dobriy Den!* (Good day!) is "*Як картопля? Вже викопали?*" ("How are the potatoes? Did you finish digging them?") In March the question is, "Did you sort your potatoes yet (for planting)?" but in July it is, "Did the Colorado bugs eat all of your potatoes? What poison are you using?" We are straight talkers, we don't even say pesticides, we say poison. How is it that I ended up talking about potatoes again? I tell you, everything eventually ends up being about potatoes for poor Ukrainian villagers. Even if you have left the village, the village has not left you.

Now (after 24 years of living in the U.S.) I am so used to how people respond to "How are you?" that I begin to expect it. Even more so, I get a bit surprised or taken aback when the answer to the question, "How are you?" is answered with "Lousy. My personal life is a dumpster fire, and my business is taking a nosedive." or "I feel very lonely. It's hard to live alone in this big empty house all by myself." In the Midwest, whenever I ask someone, "How are you?" a common reply is "Okay," but it often actually means the opposite, that they are not okay. When giving them time to respond, they will open up if the relationship allows for it. Can you imagine how much confusion this creates to people new to this way of communicating?

During my first years in the U.S., when people ask me, "How are you?" I take it as a real question, not a greeting. So, these unsuspecting people stand there and hear me tell my life story when all they thought they were saying was "Hi." I proceed to tell them how I am and it doesn't faze me at all that they don't really mean it that way. At the same time, I meet people who truly care about my well-being and who ask how I'm doing, ready to hear the good, the bad, and the ugly. I learn that meanings are created in context and are not static as the grammar books position language to be.

Spectrum of Politeness: From Brutally Honest to Beating Around the Bush

I learn that I am perceived as a rude person when I'm transplanted to the Midwest. It comes to me as a surprise because, in my heart, I am not trying to be rude. I consider myself kind, polite, and respectful. My parents, my relatives, my teachers, and my community raised me to be that way. I still hear the voice of my teachers saying *"Слухай уважно!"* ("Listen attentively!"). My parents said to use the polite pronoun ви (you) when addressing people respectfully. My community prioritized and taught us not to be selfish and to think of the needs of others and respect our elders. My mom's strongest value was hospitality with this rule: If a guest comes in, give up your softest bed and put out the best spread of food for them. My people also valued telling the truth to the people you love, even if it hurts to hear it. Because our government lied so much to us, we cherish truth and honesty more than gold.

Rob likes taking me to the mall. That's how we spend our time together before the kids come. We don't have money to spend, so we just do a lot of window shopping. We are in Sunglass Hut. I pick up a pair, look at the price and tell Rob, "These are overpriced." The saleswoman most likely hears me. Later, Rob pulls me aside outside the store and whispers to me, "Honey, that's rude. We don't say things like that in front of the people who work there." My response is, "Nonsense. It's the truth, isn't it? Why would you charge $300 for a pair of shades? Why can't I tell her that they are overpriced?" I realize I'm construed as being defensive, but I'm not, really, because all I'm trying to do is justify my reasoning. Being evaluated as rude by my closest family members hurts because I am not trying to be rude in any way, shape, or form. I can't blame them because that's how they are used to communicating. They didn't grow up in Ukraine where rudeness and politeness are construed differently.

When I say at the checkout register that their machine must be broken, my language and attitude are interpreted as rude (as I was told after the fact). Or when I don't hold the door on my way out of the mall for the person behind me, that's considered rude. I am familiar with the practice of holding the door for someone to go in, especially men holding the door for women or the elderly. But in America, I learn this is a no-no because women are equals here and to indicate to an elderly person that they are elderly is borderline ageism. I must be a slower learner, I tell myself because I just figured this out about a year ago. I walk out of a mall and let the door close behind me. A woman is following me out, and I am pretty sure both of her hands were fully functional, but she accuses me of being rude by saying "Excuse YOU!" The accusation hurts, and to me, her behavior is more rude than mine, but I know I'm wrong because I forgot to hold the door for her.

These are the unspoken rules that no book on American culture ever writes about because people are not aware they exist, and also because they are unique to particular places and situations. I wonder how door etiquette is handled in New York or overcrowded places like buses. I wonder if my behavior is less rude in those places. I realize that if foreigners aren't insightful or quick enough to figure them out on their own, then we are considered rude.

Telling the truth about overpriced sunglasses is considered honest in Ukraine but rude in the Midwest. In the Midwest, people use indirect communication from making requests to declining an invitation. I've compiled a list of phrases in the table below as examples of indirect communication.

Table I. Examples of Indirect Communication.

What People Say in the Midwest	What I Used to Think It Meant	What It Actually Means (When Spoken Indirectly)
"Let me know if I can do anything."	Let me know if I can do anything.	I hope you never ask me for help.
"I'll keep that in mind."	I'll keep that in mind.	That's the dumbest thing I ever heard.
"I wish I could go."	She regrets she can't go.	I have no interest in going.
"Something came up."	An emergency came up, I hope everyone is okay!	How can I get out of this invitation?
"That's different" in response to "How did you like that meal?"	That's different from anything I've ever eaten before.	This tastes horrible.
"That's interesting."	That's a very interesting idea. She must be a genius.	I hate it.
Let's do coffee soon!	Let's have coffee tomorrow!	It's not happening!
"Thanks a lot!"	She is so thankful, my heart is full!	I don't really feel thankful at all.

What People Say in the Midwest	What I Used to Think It Meant	What It Actually Means (When Spoken Indirectly)
"That's okay," in response to "I saved a cookie for you."	Good, as in agreement.	I don't want your cookie.
"That's unique/ creative."	Wow! I'm Van Gogh!	That's the ugliest thing I've seen. This kid has no talent.

It doesn't mean these phrases can't be taken literally, such as, "I am honestly busy." The meaning of these phrases is dependent on the context of the situation, particularly on the relationship between people.

But why do people use indirect communication versus direct? My latest theory is that it's about values. In Ukraine, we value honesty. Communicating directly means communicating honestly and not responding to "How do you like the soup?" with a white lie, like "not bad," which actually means "this soup takes like nothing." In Ukraine, we say things like "not enough salt" or "not enough spices" in an effort to improve the soup. For us, it's about the quality of feedback. My guess is that indirect communicators value politeness over hurting other people's feelings.

For direct communicators, truth and honesty are more important than appearing to be polite. Direct communicators do not consider themselves rude. Even among people who don't speak the truth directly at first, sometimes they will speak candidly and honestly after a sufficient level of trust has been developed with the person they are speaking to, leading to a stronger and more sincere relationship. Speaking of values, in Minnesota there is the ubiquitous "Minnesota Nice," attitude, a characteristic of the Minnesota culture. Being direct and valuing honesty rubs against the grain of "Minnesota Nice" like nails on a chalkboard.

When we host Japanese students, I learn that indirectness is on a spectrum. If Ukrainians are on the far left side of the spectrum of directness, and Minnesotans are in the middle, then the Japanese would be on the far right side. When the Japanese students refuse cupcakes because they are too sweet, they don't say "No, thank you." Saying "No" to something is considered too direct. Instead, they say, "Too much sugar." and "Maybe, not so much."

Those who work with Japanese people will agree that they communicate more indirectly than Midwesterners, valuing politeness over quality feedback. The concept of *honne* and *tatemae* create a sometimes confusing course of communication with Japanese people, because they have learned to say what is accepted by societal norms (*tatemae*) and which is generally very polite, rather than to speak their minds honestly (*honne*), which can be misconstrued as being impolite.

There is definitely a spectrum of directness versus indirectness. Neither of the approaches is wrong. What's important is understanding the cultural approaches. This understanding can ultimately lead to having a better understanding of people and not judging individuals, attributing it to their personality.

Unspoken Rules About Polite Communication

I notice that the Minnesotan way of communicating also influences how people make requests. In fact, there is a spectrum of directness when requests are made. On one end of the spectrum is the most indirect such as, "It's stuffy in here," or not saying anything as not to offend people or insinuate that the quality of air is not good. In the middle is, "Do you think you could … I'm wondering if … Would you be so kind as to open a window … If it's not too much to ask."

Then at the other end of the spectrum is, "Do you mind if I open the window?" This is rarely heard because it's considered impolite to be in charge of someone else's windows and air temperature when not in one's own home. On the extreme end of the spectrum is something you never hear in the Midwest because it is outright rude. "Open the window, please." Even "please" does not soften the blow of such directness. I suspect that there's even a more rude form for angry people such as, "Open the darn window!" But I never hear that in real life because people don't yell or show emotions in public in the land of the Minnesota nice.

Many rules about politeness are communicated explicitly and others are implicit, and I have to figure them out on my own. The explicit rules mandate that you have to say "Please" and "Thank you." I understand that it's appropriate to say this to a 4-year-old kid, but as a 22-year-old, it feels like I am being treated like a child and as if I don't know how to be polite at this age.

For example, I say with a polite tone in my voice, "Can I have an apple?" and am corrected to say, "Can I have an apple, please." I was raised to be polite, but politeness is construed differently in different cultures. In Ukraine, we do say "thank you," but we don't use it casually like some Americans do when they say "Thanks" or "Thanks a lot," which can be taken sarcastically, as in "Thanks, but no thanks." In Ukraine, please is not a required word because the tone of voice can communicate politeness. "You are welcome" is rarely used, not because we are not polite people, but because we have other ways of showing our appreciation. In fact, the words for "Please" and "You are welcome" are the same: *будь ласка*, which means "be kind."

Because I am a linguist, I constantly analyze language. I notice how requests are made using the phrase "Thank you." For example, "Thank you for not loitering," "Thank you for picking up after your dog," "Thank you for not smoking," "Thank you for returning your cart." Linguistically, these are requests and not words of appreciation. They are ways of making requests in a polite manner. We don't want to be rude by saying, "The second-hand smoke from your disgusting habit could cause cancer in other people." That would be too much text for a sign, don't you think? Polite society wouldn't accept "Don't just leave your shopping cart in the middle of the parking lot, you lazy cretin. Put it in the cart corral," but it would be humorous to try, don't you think?

I also learn about different ways of saying "No" to refuse something. There is a spectrum from less to more polite. We don't just say "No," we should say "No, thank you," but even that's too direct. I learn from my kids when they say, "I'm good," it means they don't want something. "Do you want some carrots?" "I'm good," Julian says. "Are you sure?" "Yep."

It takes me decades to interpret and make these requests in a Minnesota-nice way. It's because learning another language is learning another culture. We don't just take words from one language and translate them into another. I try that for the first five years in the U.S. and fail every time. That's what Google Translate is for. When you communicate in another culture's language, you have to learn how to say things in the way of that culture within a particular context, not just translate your words into their language word for word.

The word-for-word communication is common, especially at the beginning stages of learning a new language. But what surprises me the most is when it continues on after decades of communicating in a new language. For example, I say to Rob, "Honey, can you warm up the water for me?" I'm supposed to say, "Honey, I'd like some tea. Would you mind boiling some water for me?" I also learn that the use of "could" is more polite than "can" as in "Could you please put the kettle on?" versus "Can you please put the kettle on?" But in Ukrainian, we simply say "Put the kettle on." I hear my mom's voice as I write these words and they sound polite and gentle without the "please" and "could you" and "do you mind?"

With time, I become so skilled at making requests fitting the Midwestern norms that even my own honey Rob has a hard time getting the message because I make requests so indirectly. I say to him, "The tea bag is already in the cup." Jokingly, he asks, "And what do you want me to do with it?"

I hear American parents say to their kids, "Would you like to put your shoes on?" "Would you like to lose your phone privileges now or in an hour?" "Sweetie, it's time to get dressed." Yeah, right, I can hear the kids say, "Sure, Mommy, take my phone privileges away now. I don't want to wait a whole hour!" or "Yes, of course, I'd like to put my shoes on. Thank you for giving me a chance, Mommy. I love you forever."

I am amazed at these requests uttered by most middle-class moms for two reasons. One, they are stated as choices but in reality, they are commands. Second, these requests aren't effective, but that's the language of requests I hear ubiquitously. Typically, this progression happens: "Sweetie, make sure you have your shoes on. You don't want your feet to get cold, do you?" to "Please put your shoes on!" "Sweetie, please get dressed. PLEASE." Then it escalates to "PUT. YOUR. SHOES. ON!!" dragging the kid with one shoe on and strapping him into the car seat while snapping at the kid and putting his own shoes on. From choices to shouting commands in three easy steps.

In the way Mom communicates with me, there is no ambiguity in her requests. She utters two to four words like, "Comb your hair," or "Don't rip your dress." It doesn't mean I obeyed her. I'm just saying how requests are formed. They always start with a verb, "Pick up your toys," or "Clean up this mess," and not "Sweetie, you made such a mess. Let's see how quickly you can turn that messy room into a lovely place where we can hang out later!" Most American kids are conditioned from early on to understand indirect communication. This also speaks to very different patterns of child rearing in which children are positioned as beings capable of making wise choices early on.

I travel back to my childhood where, as a child, I am given orders and not choices. I am 4 years old and my mom tells me if I don't listen to my sister, Baba Yaga will come and eat me. I quickly hurry up because I know that

Baba Yaga is always hungry and she has an enormous appetite for naughty children. I know that she has a clever helper, Olenka, and the two of them are always on the lookout for naughty children.

When the Baba Yaga threats lose their power, then Mom transitions to threatening me with some mythical creature at the bottom of the well. Our well is two feet away from our house, which makes the danger imminent and I am scared to death. When I am in school, teachers play a more direct role in our rearing and inspire us to be like Lenin. Behaving like Lenin means obeying and not needing reminders. If you need reminders and you disobey authority, you will not be promoted from Octobryonok to Young Pioneers. No teacher asks us, "Do Young Pioneers behave this way?"

"Just wanted to follow up ..." and other sayings of professional emails

Many of my fellow non-native English speakers concur that it is difficult to craft messages indirectly and understand people when messages are spoken indirectly. I make an effort to learn how to adjust my language from being too direct to being more indirect because I realize that my success depends on my flexibility of adapting my communication style. On a good day, when I have lots of positive energy, I successfully use the motto "be all things to all people," like the Apostle Paul said when preaching the Gospel to different people. So I try to be a Ukrainian to Ukrainians and a Midwesterner to Midwesterners. I also learn that too much honesty said without love can be damaging to relationships, so I try to be guided by the biblical wisdom to "speak the truth in love." But I'm never perfect, and I am reminded that I am a work in progress.

In the workplace, indirect communication takes on a different shape. I spend many hours revising my emails just to fit the cultural expectations of my workplace and the people I communicate with. I call it a sandwich approach. I start with asking how they've been or saying, "I hope they enjoyed your weekend," or, "I hope this email finds you well," or how lovely it was to see them at the meeting. Then I make the point I was originally writing the email for. Then I close it with something like, "Let's revisit this later," which is another way of saying, "Goodbye, hope we never have to bring this issue up again." If I need to remind people, then I employ the phrase, "Just wanted to follow up." Politeness is of utmost importance even if the communication is not sincere when using phrases such as, "Thought I'd check to see how you're doing," or "With all due respect."

In many conversations via email and face-to-face modes, I notice that people in the Midwest are afraid to say "No" directly. Instead, they say, "Let me think about that," or "Let's revisit that later," or "Not sure if that's going to work," or "Let me see what I can do." For many years I interpret these phrases literally and often get surprised when the person will come back and say, "We already had that discussion and decided it's not going to work." But because I took the phrases literally, I didn't interpret them as decisions or rejections. You can see how that can lead to some major misunderstandings. What's even worse is when I use a phrase like, "Let me see what I can do," literally, but notice that people interpret it figuratively. So I often have to add, "I mean literally."

Another email line I'm most likely overusing is, "I'm wondering if …" Honestly, no one is wondering. Whoever uses the line, "I'm wondering," already knows the answer. Again, I'm using my honesty lens here to judge this indirect communication. I find that indirect communication is time-consuming, can be misleading, and tries to cushion the receiver from the brunt of the main message. So, for the immigrant, it's double the work when interpreting the message.

As I'm writing this book, I ask my friends on Facebook for examples of indirect messages. Some of the ones they share are new to me because this whole time I thought they meant exactly what they said. One of them is, "Something came up." I always interpret that as "An emergency came up." Only when someone explains to me that this is often used as an excuse, I now understand what it means when used indirectly. In a genuine relationship, your friend won't be vague about it, but will tell you about the emergency if there really is one that came up that interfered with your plans.

But a bit too much directness makes me long for the indirect style, especially when I go back to Ukraine and my aunt tells me, "Wow, you've gained weight."

Small Talk Paralysis

In the dental office:

> *"Anything bothering you with your teeth?"*
>
> *"Nope."*
>
> *"So, how are the kids?"*
>
> *"Great, thanks."*
>
> *"So, what are you guys planning for spring break?"*

It takes me awhile to say something in response to that because I just don't feel like I need to share my spring break or summer vacation or Christmas plans with my dental hygienist. I'm guessing they are trained to make the patient comfortable and put them at ease because most Americans hate going to the dentist. But for me, going to a dentist in America is like going to a spa because I had endured 20 years of Ukrainian dentistry—15 years of top notch Soviet dental care and five years of free socialized medical care in independent Ukraine. One time, the dentist ran out of Novocain, so he pulled my tooth, expecting me to be a Spartan. Don't complain in front of me of getting a paper cut. Even my dad cried as he sat next to me during the procedure. If they really want to put me at ease, I prefer Novocain over small talk.

In the elevator:

"Hi, how are you doing? How was your weekend?"

"Great. We were having cabin fever, so I took the kids skiing. Felt good to get out. And yours?" I reply in a good mood, doing the American thing.

"Low key. Got some stuff done around the house, ran some errands, did the laundry."

"Yeah, the never-ending laundry."

These are my least favorite conversations that usher in my week at work. The small talk happens in break room chats, elevator rides (and my office is on the 12th floor!), and kicking off business meetings. I know they're important. I participate in them. I start them … rarely, but I do so because it's an expectation. Silence is dreadful. Weather and sports are safe to talk about. (Unless you are in Wisconsin and say that you are happy that the Packers lost and the Vikings won. Then it's not safe, so you have to just smile and lie about your allegiance.)

I compare small talk to my workout warm-up. For a half-hour cardio work-out, I need a two- to three-minute warm-up. You don't want to jump into a heart-pumping workout without warming up your muscles. Small talk to me is the same. Your brain muscles can't jump straight into business without a warm-up.

In the Ukrainian culture, if you start a discussion with small talk, people will think you are being fake or that you are trying to avoid something.

So, the next time I see you, if I ask, "How are you?" I really mean it. When you invite me over for a coffee and I say, "My son has a basketball game," that means my son indeed has a basketball game on Saturdays, but I can do coffee in the afternoon. If you ask me how the cake was, I won't say, "That's different." Instead, I might say, "too much sugar for my taste," but

I will say it politely.

And if I see you in an elevator, you have my permission to stand there very quietly and enjoy the moment without feeling pressured to ask me about my weekend. When I come to work, I'm geared up for the week and leave my weekend behind to discuss with my family over dinner. And, finally, if you see me sandwiching my emails, just tell me, "Ru, you can be as direct with me as you like." And when I say, "Let me know if I can do anything," in response to, "I hurt my back," that means I can come over tonight and help you vacuum the house and do your dishes or bring you dinner. But if you see me and ask, "How are you?" be prepared for a 15-minute response. If I respond with the phrase, "Fine, thank you, and you?" then I have finally mastered the art of American small talk, and it is just fine for you to respond with, "Good, thank you," and carry on your merry little way.

Public Dress Codes

I get my first paycheck in 1997 and buy myself a $250 Wilson's leather jacket. I am living my college dream of having money and wearing leather—the dream I couldn't achieve being a poor college student. I buy new shoes, high heels, of course, and wear them to the grocery store. I have my high heels on, a dress, and a nice trench coat. I look around and notice that people are dressed casually and that I'm overdressed. Over time, I get more relaxed with my clothes and appearance. Sometimes I run into the store after my workout and discover no one cares that I'm dressed in leggings and a sweaty T-shirt. In the U.S., there isn't as much pressure about one's public appearance. Through various observations and experiences, I learn that there are unspoken rules about dress in public, and as it is with language, it's all about context.

We make language choices in the context of a particular culture and in a particular situation (purpose, audience, and mode of communication) and we make clothing choices based on the context of culture and the context of situation. For example, I learn that sweatpants are okay for Walmart, but you need to dress better for Target (according to guests on The Tonight Show with Jay Leno). Piggly Wiggly can tolerate greasy hair, but for Byerly's or Metcalf's (upscale grocery stores), a shower and makeup are more apropos. Here are some of my observations of dress codes in the Midwest. These rules are followed by some people and broken by others.

- Don't wear the same clothes two days in a row. Especially tops. I wear the same black pants or skirt for two days in a row, but I change my tops every day. I remember my college days of owning only two tops and wearing them twice a week.

- Black and blue don't go together. Don't wear a blue top with black pants. If you do, people will think you don't have good lighting in your closet.

- Don't wear green and red together once Christmas is over. Green and red are Christmas colors. Period. I learn this one when people give me looks when I show up at a professional development meeting in a green blazer and a red turtleneck on January 6th. The famous linguist Stephen Krashen came to Minnesota, so I dressed to the nines!

- Wear white (especially pants) only after Memorial Day and never after Labor Day. I intentionally buy a white denim jacket and start wearing it in April. Rob says, "You are such a rebel!"

- Don't dress up for grocery stores. Sweatpants are okay. If you wear heels, makeup, and fancy coats or clothing, it means you are stopping by to pick up a bottle of wine or dessert on your way to a party.

- No need to dress up for middle-level restaurants. In the early years, I find myself overdressed for Perkins, Applebee's, or Olive Garden.

- If you live in Wisconsin, wearing shorts in 40-degree weather doesn't mean you don't own warm pants. To a Ukrainian, it's a sure sign of parental neglect and that your child will catch a cold.

- Don't wear real fur on liberal college campuses where animal rights activists protest against animal abuse. You could get egged. If you wear fake fur, make sure it looks really fake.

- Deodorant is required. Body odor is not tolerated, unless you are in the gym, but even then ...

- Unless you are going for an interview, ironing is optional if you remember to take clothes out of the dryer before they get wrinkled. I find freedom in that. I get flashbacks to childhood when my mom made me iron my underwear and sheets to kill the germs. We didn't have a dryer. We survived somehow.

- Women have to work harder than men at their appearance. If a guy shows up disheveled, it speaks to his brilliance, but if a woman does, it means she ran out the door chasing the kids with a bowl of cereal in her hands making sure the kids eat breakfast. That double standard rule seems to be universal but no one talks about it, so it is a universal unspoken rule rooted in sexism.

I learn that these are important rules to live by and if you break them, you do it at your own peril. One of these days, I'll show up in the same top two days in a row and watch what happens. Or I'll come with messy hair and say something brilliant and redefine the whole double standard of the "Messy Male" tolerance. But I realize I'm being too naive.

CHAPTER 10

"What Did You Eat in Ukraine?"

Land and People Interdependence

Ukraine is an agrarian country with rich and fertile land. Ukrainian farmers grow up in a symbiotic relationship with the land. We eat what's growing in our fields. There is an interdependence in this relationship. Without needing T-shirts or having bumper stickers that say, "Eat local," or "Locally sourced," we live according to the following value as growers of our own food: you take care of the earth, and the earth will take care of you. My dad knows how to cultivate and fertilize the soil, and rotate crops. We raise animals and they help with fertilization.

Our diet is based on what each season provides. The cuisine is quite simple, with bread, grains, and potatoes being the main staples. We also enjoy fresh vegetables in the summer months and root vegetables in the fall and winter that we store in the root cellar. The root cellar is underground where the frost rarely reaches when the temperatures dip below freezing.

As a child, I spend a quarter of my time in the root cellar, either putting things away for storage or bringing them out for cooking and eating. We have shelves lined with canned vegetables and fruit. My favorite food to get out of the cellar in the cold winter is canned apples and compote (cherry and berry mix). They are firmly packed in a sugary syrup and we eat them for dessert in the winter. During bitter cold winters, my sister and I take turns

Canned berry compote in a sugary syrup.

descending the stone steps to bring a 3-liter glass jar upstairs so we can enjoy sweet juicy apples after each meal.

Spring is the leanest time for food options. The canned food in the root cellar is picked over. All the sugary apples are gone. The best jams are eaten. Fresh beets, carrots, and potatoes begin to shrivel up. It's the season in-between. There is no fresh fruit to speak of besides shriveled-up apples. Portions of the apples begin to rot and we cut them off and eat the rest.

I watch some Americans eat only half of the apple around the core and throw away the rest and I remember how we ate even the apple core, sparing only the stem and seeds. Not because we were poor, but because we didn't throw away any food. "Enjoy every last bite," I say to myself. I still, to this day, eat apples all the way down to the seeds. If dad buys apples or oranges, he never eats any. He saves everything for the kids because "Kids need vitamins," he says. Even when we visit in the summer from America and Rob buys bananas and peaches, Dad is used to saving exotic fruit for the kids. He never develops a taste for bananas.

The meat we eat is from the animals we raise on our farm. A pig is butchered in early December when the temps are colder so that the meat won't spoil as quickly. But the main reason is that by December the pig is nice and plump. I cover my ears so I don't hear it squeal when the neighbor and my dad cut its throat in our backyard. Then they use a blow torch to burn the hair off the pig. My mom's dad, Grandpa Ivan (Ee-vahn) was a local expert at butchering pigs. Butchering is a man's job in Ukraine.

The women spend at least three days cleaning, cooking, and preserving the meat. Using pig intestines, we make regular sausage, blood sausage, *saltison* (another kind

Aunt Lida and Uncle Vanya (my dad's brother).

of sausage), and other delicacies like cooked tongue, heart, and liver. December is a month-long feast! The women cook and stew and can, and day after day, we eat freshly cooked pork products. The smell fills the air in the entire yard because the cooking and canning happen in the summer kitchen. Mom brings us plates full of sausages into the house from the summer kitchen and we eat until our bellies are full.

We also eat chickens, goats, rabbits, and ducks. Duck meat is too heavy for my taste. I prefer rabbit. Rabbit is considered among Ukrainians as some of the most "dietary" meat: it is lean and nutritious. My Tyotya Lida (Dad's sister) always makes stewed rabbit whenever I come to visit. She stews a broth so savory, the meat falls right off the bones.

We butcher our own chickens and throw the chicken heads to our dog, Barsik, to eat. Ukrainian farmers don't fall for the old wives' tale that you can't give chicken bones to your dog. My mom teaches me how to pluck the chickens, but I am never taught how to chop their heads off. That's Dad's job. They wiggle too much. Chickens' brains are really small, so when you chop their heads off, their bodies just keep going. That is too much for my young, sensitive eyes.

All our chickens are "free range" and their eggs are "cage free," produced by free-roaming chickens. Our dairy products are pasture-raised, not pasteurized. I am amused when it becomes trendy in the U.S. to buy free-range chickens and cage-free eggs. To me, that is the only way chickens ever existed. When I get nostalgic for the free-range chickens of my childhood, I drive over to the chicken farmer on the other side of town, say hello to his chickens, and buy my cage-free eggs.

Nicky feeding the goat that my parents later made stew out of, June 2017.

We never name our goats and chickens. We eat them. I know, we're barbarians. One summer Nicky and Julian visit my parents and really enjoy playing with this kid. And by kid, I mean our baby goat. Being American city boys, they treat the goat like it's their pet. I think Nicky even named him. So, when we return to the U.S. and Skype my parents later in the fall, Nicky asks how the baby goat is doing. Dad says, "We ate him." I see Nicky's face slowly grow pale in shock. How could you eat my baby goat?

We also eat the fish that the river provides. The best ones are about the length of your index finger. We deep fry the small *ribka* after dipping them into egg and flour batter and ate them with their heads still on. They are so small, we can't even feel the bones when we crunch on the deep fried goodness. As one American leader Donna Sahlin told me after being served fish in Ukraine, "I couldn't eat it. The eyes were still looking at me." During my first year in Minnesota, I discover that fish are caught for entertainment, an odd idea to Ukrainians.

Ron, my host dad, and I are fishing on Crooked Lake. I'm so excited that I catch my first fish in a frozen lake (probably a crappie). And I do it fast before my behind freezes to the chair. I have a picture to prove it (the fish, not my frozen behind). I eagerly get this fabulous idea of introducing something Ukrainian to my host family and decide to make fish soup out of it, but Ron lets the fish go, which is another area of confusion. Why in the world would you let a fish go after you catch it? What's the point of fishing then? Catch and release? In my childhood, we caught fish and fried it—heads, eyes, and all.

Anyhoo (or is it moreover?), we end up making fish soup out of frozen fish, not from the frozen lake but from the freezer. It is halibut Ron caught in Alaska and shipped to Minnesota. Why would you ship fish from Alaska, if you have a lake full of bottom feeder crappies and an occasional walleye? I make my first fish soup for my American host family in Minnesota and proudly serve it. Ron says, "That's different." By now I know what that means. I also know they don't ask me to make fish soup again.

Soup's On!

In the house where I grow up, our weekly dinner menu consists mainly of soups. In addition to soups, we eat potatoes, salads, and seasonal vegetables and fruit. The ingredients and variety of soups change through the seasons. In winter, salads are replaced by pickled tomatoes or pickled cucumbers (called pickles in the U.S.), and soups are replaced by жаркое (*zharkoye or* stew)*,* and капусняк *(kapusniak,* sauerkraut "soup") with millet and mashed potatoes. Here is a typical weekly menu:

Monday: Buckwheat soup
Tuesday: Millet soup
Wednesday: Borsch

Thursday: Macaroni soup or fried potatoes and eggs

Friday: Mashed potatoes with gravy and some meat

Saturday: Borsch (If it were up to Dad, he'd have borsch three times a week.)

Sunday: Buckwheat kasha with *kotleti* (flattened meatballs made with ground pork.)

Special meals on weekends were *vareniki* (called pierogis in the US). They can sweet or savory. Sweet *vareniki* are filled with seasonal berries: cherries, strawberries, plums – whatever grows in the garden. Savory *vareniki* are made with potatoes, sourkraut, or cheese. My favorite kind is cherry vareniki. Mom always makes them steamed, not boiled (a regional difference). She wraps a cheesecloth over the pot and places each carefully, without touching. They rise with the steam from the boiling water and the dough is very light and fluffy.

Traditional classic holiday meals: cabbage rolls, *kholodets* (aspic), vinaigrette salad, *olivye* salad, pork cutlets, herring and red beet salad called *shuba* (fur coat).

Mom making vareniki. Summer 2017.

For breakfast, my dad has two small meals. The first is tea and bread with jam and butter, early in the morning before everyone is awake, because my dad always wakes up before the rest of us. Then a second breakfast, which is usually leftovers from the meal the night before or an omelet, but never by itself, rather with other food like cut-up summer sausage.

All meals are interchangeable in Ukraine. There is no such thing as separate breakfast foods in Ukraine, like cereal and pancakes. We do make pancakes and oatmeal but we can eat those any time of day. We also make omelets, but serve *kovbasa,* or leftover cutlets, from the day before to make sure breakfast is a hearty meal because we don't eat lunch until 2 p.m. I am surprised at American breakfasts and refuse to eat cereal packed with sugar. As a child, I remember running around the house with a small box of frosted corn flakes and just eating them dry by reaching with my hand inside the box, grabbing handfuls, dropping some on the floor and hearing my mom, "Don't scatter corn flakes. Clean up after yourself!"

In the summer, food is fresh from the garden, and prepared simply. There is often a salad for breakfast, such as cabbage salad or cucumber and tomato salad with some sunflower oil drizzled over. In the U.S., I still don't eat American salad dressings. I switched over to olive or avocado oil after several years of trying to find an oil that works well by itself (without the added garlic and pepper) on salads. American grocery stores don't carry sunflower oil that meets my expectations. It has to be unrefined and super flavorful. I can smell it as I'm writing this. Have you ever seen sunflower fields in Ukraine? We grow sunflowers like Iowans grow corn! Sometimes, when I'm desperate, I go to a European Deli where they carry products from the "former Soviet republics."

From Soups to Sandwiches

One of the ways immigrants first discover they're in a new land is through the food. My initial adjustment is to switch from a liquid, soupy diet to dry foods. Instead of soups and borsch, there are dry sandwiches between two slices of bread that are soft and mushy. I am used to open-faced sandwiches on hearty bread with a thin slice of summer sausage or salami and a slice of fresh cucumber. Instead of borsch, there are burgers and pizza.

It takes a couple of weeks for me to adjust to solid food, my stomach aching during that time. I also notice that American restaurants serve larger portions than what I ate at home. When I go out to eat for the first time in the U.S., I order a salad and a cheeseburger because I like good cheese, but I didn't know what a cheeseburger was. I thought it was just a bun with cheese in it. The salad fills up the entire salad plate with large chunks of lettuce. I stare at the chunky lettuce and remember how my mom taught me to shred cabbage finely because large chunks mean you are in a hurry and careless.

The burger is yet another challenge. It is so tall I can't open my mouth wide enough to put it in, plus I am used to open-faced sandwiches. So I take off the top slice of the bun and cut the burger in pieces like our *kotletki* at home. The buns remind me of булочки (*bulochki*), which we eat with jam and tea, sort of like sweet brioche bread. I end up with a huge portion of food untouched. I never order a cheeseburger again. Not to this day.

My dad does the same thing with the burger when I make it for him here in the States. He eats the first one trying to open his mouth wide, his jaw almost clicking and locking. When he has leftovers the next day, he asks me if it would be rude to cut it up into pieces and eat it with ketchup, and make a salad with the lettuce, but chop it finer like a chopped salad. My dad and I just don't have the jaw muscles for burgers.

But then I discover a variety of veggie burgers at SmashBurger, a new hamburger joint in Roseville, Minnesota. They are juicier than just a beef burger and have more ingredients in them than just lettuce and tomato. I expose my taste buds to Avocado Ranch Black Bean Burger; Spicy Jalapeno Baja Burger; Spinach, Cucumber and Goat Cheese Bean Burger, and a whole lot more. I embrace the avocado veggie burgers and when I eat them, I feel more American.

I am in an American grocery store in the bread aisle. The bread aisle always smells like chemicals. I can't quite get used to it. It has the same effect as when you walk into Michael's (a craft store) and get a headache-inducing blast of dry potpourri and eucalyptus that almost knocks me off my feet. These are the earliest smells I notice that are new to me in the U.S.: the smell of potpourri at Michael's and the smell of chemicals in the bread aisle.

The bread in the U.S. never goes stale. Mold eventually grows on it, after about three weeks, but it never goes stale, not like fresh bread does. And it is so soft and malleable, that it would be considered to be a sign of poor quality in Ukraine. We have a saying that the bread is so soft, you can mold it into коники (*koniky or* ponies). Think about a loaf of the hearty and dense German pumpernickel (not American pumpernickel). You can't bend it, let alone make *koniky* out of it.

But as an immigrant, I am warned not to be critical of the negative things I discover in my cultural observations. Otherwise, people would say, "If you don't like it, then you can go back home." But a critique can be healthy as long as it doesn't turn to America bashing and seeing only flaws. I love many things about the U.S. and find others that are not to my taste. I also find American bakeries within grocery stores and a variety of breads I didn't know existed. I discover French baguettes, sourdough, ciabatta, focaccia, brioche, and I'm in love with America again. America provides such an efficient way to taste bread from all over the world. I'm thankful to immigrants who brought their breads and seasonings, and their entire cuisines with them when they immigrated here.

During the first three months in the U.S., I am in a delirious state. Some call it the honeymoon stage. I'm not sure if I'm awake or if I'm dreaming. Everything is so new and so wonderful! I call it the fairy-tale stage. During this stage, I find everything about America to be awesome, even its preservative-packed wheat bread that comes in a bag with a label "may contain wheat," and a chicken soup that comes out of a packet.

Later, after the honeymoon delirium wears off, I am in a state of cultural hangover. I am a bit conflicted because I still think positive thoughts about America but I am beginning to notice things that bother me, a sort of cognitive dissonance. Wait a minute, how can I love this country and see problems at the same time? How can those two thoughts coexist in my head? The conflict is compounded by the fact that I am supposed to believe that America is great and everything is better here. So, I start believing it. As a result, I begin to internalize that everything is superior in America and that things in Ukraine aren't as good, including the food I grew up with.

I am happy when I discover that my American family loves borsch. They also make wonderful homemade bread. That's a win-win! I remember once trying to make *plov*, an Uzbek meal, which requires an inch of oil for the rice cooker where I was going to cook rice and other vegetables. It's criticized as being too greasy and I never try to make *plov* again. Yet, I think that potato chips, burgers, fries, and pepperoni pizza are greasier, especially when they are super-sized.

I remember my mom telling me that in the Buzhanka store, they started selling *чипси*, potato chips. She said that she was appalled that parents even let their children eat the chips! When I learn to be critical of the Ukrainian food I grew up with, I start telling my parents to stop eating greasy food and start eating healthier. I tell my mom to throw away her jar of pork lard she loves to cook with and I police their food choices. Six months later she dies. Not from a coronary, but from breast cancer.

I regret being the enlightened American that I am. I regret that some of the last conversations I have with her are me telling her to change her eating habits. I do preface it by saying, "I care about you, Mom, and that's why I'm telling you to throw away the jar of lard." No matter how well I try to justify it, now in hindsight, I think it was just stupid, with a capital *S*, to say that. That's the danger of emigrating and being "enlightened" and having a clinical approach to food and life—we think we know better than the people who never left. What's worse is that according to the Keto diet, we are not eating enough fat. So, I guess even *salo* and lard in moderation are okay.

Negotiating Cross-Cultural Cooking

When I marry Rob, a red-blooded carnivore, I have to learn how to cook as if I had never cooked before. It's like going back to kindergarten to learn how to read, but you are 18. Buckwheat soup on Monday and a millet soup on Tuesday ain't gonna work. I even try an "American" grain, like quinoa, and make soup with it. Yum! If you are a soup lover, I'll be happy to share my favorite recipe for quinoa chicken soup with you.

When I marry Rob, I learn that for him a meal means a hunk of meat and potatoes on the side. Potatoes are my saving grace. I know potatoes. But in Ukraine, we grew up eating meat with the bone on, the way it comes from the animal: chicken meat comes on the bone, pork meat comes on the bone, even fish comes on the bone, lots of bones! So, I learn how to transition from drumsticks to chicken breasts (the ones that don't taste like chicken, as my mom said, unless they are cage free and free range). I learn how to transition from just enough meat to flavor the gravy to meat being the main thing on the plate.

Cooking in America means asking questions like, "What spices go together? What do you mean you don't put dill into your chicken soup? What spices go into burgers? What is that smell in chili?" I can't get used to the smell of chili powder and cumin for the longest time because they are very foreign smells to me. The same with curry and chili powder, but now I love all of them. I even love cilantro.

Rob and I are newlyweds, and I make hamburgers for Rob. I put the meal in front of him, we pray, and Rob takes his first bite of the hamburger and asks "Did you put bread in the hamburger meat? "Yes," I answer. "Isn't that what you're supposed to do?" He responds, "It is if you're making meatloaf. This is a very good meatloaf sandwich, thank you, but it's not a hamburger."

I can't understand hamburgers for the longest time. First of all, we didn't eat ground beef in my family. We actually didn't eat beef at all. We didn't like the taste of beef and it was more expensive. We ate mostly pork, chickens, and roosters from our own farm. We made котлєти (*kotleti)*, or cutlets, that were small fried pork patties, but fatter ones, not flat. But hamburgers are different. They are bigger, flatter, and less tasty. Even now, when I try to shape them, they always come out rounder and smaller than your traditional hamburger patty. When they shrink on the grill, they end up being cutlet size.

My point about all this is that you grow up with certain things and your hands retain muscle memory. But not just muscle memory, it's the memory of smells and tastes, shapes and sizes. Leaving one's own land opens up a world of culinary exploration that stretches your taste buds' comfort zone and at the same time, exposes you to new flavors. What a world of cuisine opens up before me when I discover red and green Thai curry, Lao sweet rice with mangoes, Mexican sopa de mariscos, Minnesota wild rice soup, Vietnamese pho soup, Indian lamb vindaloo, and so many others. That's why I don't often go back to buckwheat soup when I can have pho soup or Thai *tom kha* soup! But as I write this, I am hungry for buckwheat soup with parsley, potatoes, and carrots. Similar to my cultural identity that expands with new experiences, I don't replace my culinary choices with the "better ones," I expand them.

As my children grow, my cooking repertoire grows with them. I learn how to make homemade chicken nuggets, chocolate chip cookies, banana bread, Italian spaghetti and meatballs, Thai peanut stir fry, beef and broccoli stir fry, and Indian chicken tikka masala. With each holiday, I learn how to make holiday meals—au gratin potatoes, hollandaise sauce for asparagus and eggs Benedict, and ham for Easter. I learn how to make pumpkin pie, pecan pie, and a Thanksgiving Day turkey. I learn to enjoy making a variety of Christmas cookies for Christmas. My daily cooking includes learning how to make my own teriyaki sauce, my own taco seasoning, my own guacamole, and my own peanut sauce to go with a stir fry. I am thankful for the internet where I learn how to make absolutely anything I want. I even learn how to make Ukrainian foods I never knew how to cook but always loved eating. In America, my world of the culinary arts has exploded.

Why Borsch is Not Soup

Before we get to the ingredients and the recipe, we have to be on the same page about two things. First, borsch is *not* beet soup, and second, it's not soup. Beets are one ingredient out of six in borsch: meat, kidney beans, potatoes, cabbage, onions, water, dill or parsley, tomato paste, some spices (Mrs. Dash will do), and sour cream.

The reason it's not a soup is simple—because it's borsch. We don't call chili, soup, right? It's just chili. Like stew, bisque, broth, or vichyssoise, borsch is its own category. I understand why people call it soup as it's just the human brain trying to make sense of new things. We sort things into pre-existing categories and when there is no category for borsch, then it goes into the soup category. But when my mom talks about what she wants to cook this week, she says, "buckwheat soup today, millet soup tomorrow, and borsch (not borsch soup) on Wednesday." Just like borsch is not soup, we also have капусняк (*kapusnyak*) made with mashed potatoes, finely chopped sauerkraut, millet (quinoa is a great substitution), and зажарка (*zazharka), which is* sautéed onion and tomato paste, with salt and pepper added to taste.

Some say that there are as many recipes for borsch as there are cooks. Also, there are regional varieties of borsch with differences in color, ingredients, and spices. I discover that even in my own household, there are differences in how we make borsch. For the first time in 46 years, I hear that you shouldn't put carrots in borsch because they are too sweet. Do you know who I learned that from? My dad. Before my mom passed away, she was in charge of borsch. I remember her putting carrots in borsch. Now that Dad is in charge of his own borsch, he tells me that carrots make borsch too sweet and it shouldn't be sweet at all. His mom even added a tablespoon of apple cider vinegar to borsch at the end to take the sweet edge off.

A traditional borsch recipe from my family starts with the meat. Any meat will do, but we mostly use pork or chicken (preferably with the bone on, like drumsticks) and kidney beans, if you like them, soaked overnight. Then you add 1 cup cubed potatoes, add salt to taste, cook for 20 minutes, then add 1/2 cup of julienned beets and 3 to 4 cups of shredded cabbage. Do not overcook cabbage, maybe 5 minutes. The final step is to sauté onions with 2 tablespoons of tomato paste and add back to the borsch. Beets can go in at the beginning, or be grated and sauteed and then added at the very end. It depends on how red you like your borsch. By adding beets at the end, your borsch will have beet-red color. By putting them in at the beginning, you'll have orange-red borsch. It's your choice. The color of your borsch is a part of your ancestry. We inherit our family DNA and for Ukrainians, part of that DNA is the color of our borsch. But some break away from our family's way of doing things. We become borsch rebels!

Here's my rebel borsch recipe where I substitute cabbage with kale, potatoes with turnips, and onions with ramps.

> 4-6 organic, cage-free, free-range, no-GMO chicken drumsticks (optional)
> 1-2 cups of organic red beans soaked with baking soda overnight (Baking soda accelerates the softening of the dry hard bean.)
> 1 red organic beet, julienned
> 2-3 white turnips julienned (to replace potatoes)
> 4 cups of shredded kale (my favorite is Lacinato kale)
> 2 cups of shredded green cabbage (don't use purple cabbage, your borsch will look purple)
> 1/2 cup of chopped onion or ramps, or 1 cup of leeks (in the spring)
> 2 Tbsp of tomato paste sautéed with onions
> Salt and pepper to taste

In the spring, we have green borsch. It's not red, because there are no beets in the spring. The beets in the root cellar would have wilted and shriveled up by the early spring, so a new borsch was invented. Green borsch is made with chopped boiled egg, nettles (yes, stinging nettles, but when they are young, they don't sting at all), potatoes, and sour cream. It's eaten only in early spring. Summer borsch is made with new kidney beans still in a pod, young cabbage, and young potatoes.

Borshch, Borsch, Borscht, or Bortsch: Why So Many Spellings?

When food travels across the world and gets picked up by different people who speak different languages with different alphabets, the original spellings change. The same thing happens to the spelling of borsch. In this book, I choose the easiest one, which I'm sure ticked off the purists who follow all the transliteration rules. To explain the original spelling of borsch, I have to teach you four letters in the Cyrillic alphabet: Б, О, Р, Щ.

Б = B as in Bob

О = O as in Oleg

Р = R as in Rob

Щ = Shch, as in Fresh Cheese

The first three letters are easy, but spelling variations happen in the last letter for obvious reasons. I have to blame the Roman alphabet for causing so much confusion as there is no letter to represent the "shch" sound in the Roman alphabet. Indeed, you need several letters to represent that sound.

When different people try to pronounce that letter, some add the *t* sound at the end even though the original spelling has no *t*. There are only four letters, and four sounds, not five in the Ukrainian spelling. However, linguistics can explain all of this. When people pronounce words made up of sounds that don't exist in their language, their sound system tries to accommodate new sounds and make sense of them. Sometimes, we delete sounds to make new words easier to pronounce. In other instances, we add sounds. In the case of borscht, there is an insertion, phonologically speaking. Wikipedia says that borsht comes from Yiddish באָרשט (borsht). I can guess it's a what linguists call a phonotactic rule of insertion, or the human brain trying to create a sound they're familiar with, that's played out there.

Why did I choose this spelling of borsch over the other ones? To make things less distracting and easier on the eye for my reader. You can choose the spelling that works for you. My favorite spelling is…. *БОРЩ*.

Over time, I learn that the cross-cultural journey of cooking doesn't have to be only about learning, but can also be about teaching. The cross-cultural journey is a two-way street, both enriching people's lives and being enriched by theirs. One example of teaching is when I invite Americans over to teach them how to make borsch. We have a borschfest—a time of cooking and eating, and learning together. One such time is when Mom and Dad visit us in the

My mom and dad with John Sahlin peeling potatoes for vinegarette salad.

United States and Sandy McMaken (our dear friend who stayed with my parents when visiting Ukraine) is still with us. I invite them over and my mom teaches them how to make cabbage rolls, borsch, and vinegarette salad.

Now both mom and Sandy are gone, cancer took their lives. This makes these memories double special. Cross-cultural learning is in full swing in those moments of people breaking bread together.

Hungering For More Than Borsch

I get hungry for borsch, but I also hunger for speaking Ukrainian. Sometimes I go to YouTube and play a Ukrainian song or listen to a Ukrainian poet just to hear the language. Then your mouth starts moving and you want to speak it. You want to articulate the sounds the way your articulatory system was formed where vowels aren't morphing and A, E, and O make only one sound per letter A =/a/, E = /e/, and O = /o/ and there are no *W's* to get in the way of saying *V.* You don't have to think about whether it's THE story or A story. It's just story (no articles). I hunger for speaking my language.

It's March 9th, Schevchenko's birthday. Taras Hryhorovych Shevchenko is the Shakespeare of Ukraine, but more so. He is more than just a poet, but also a revolutionary. He is the symbol of the Ukrainian spirit, a major figure of the Ukrainian national revival. Every year on his birthday, people celebrate him by playing banduras (traditional stringed instruments) and reading *Kobzar*, his famous collection of poems. I am thankful to the Facebook Ukrainian community for reminding me of this celebration when videos are posted on various Ukrainian pages. I play the video of 400 bandurists performing in Lviv and I put the video on loop so it can continue playing as I get in and out of the shower. In the busyness of it all, his celebration reminds me that I am Ukrainian.

Borsch does the same for me: it makes me feel Ukrainian in my inner being. When the aroma of potatoes, beets, and dill fills our kitchen, it brings me back home to my mother's kitchen, and I wish that she was here. I taste it, and it draws me back to being a Ukrainian. Speaking Ukrainian has the same effect. It's so powerful to feel how food, music, poetry, and language reconnects us to our ethnic identity and to our homeland more than anything else. I easily get pulled into my American identity and it takes hard work to reconnect with my Ukrainian self. I'm thankful for borsch, music, poetry, and language to help me connect with my ethnic self and the place, where "my umbilical cord is buried."

CHAPTER 11

"How Did You Two Meet?"

"Are You a Mail Order Bride?"

I'm in a Russian grocery store in Saint Louis Park, Minnesota. It's 2003. Rob is wearing his black and yellow North Face jacket, which screams "I am an American." It's a dead giveaway. The Russian saleswoman looks at me at the checkout and doesn't ask, "Hi, how are you? Did you find everything okay?" Instead, she bluntly asks me, "Are you here by mail?" (*Ты по почте?*) I stand there stunned, and in that moment I was missing the indirect, beating-around-the-bush language that Minnesotans are famous for, in which people imply something but don't ask it directly.

Every time someone asks me how I got here, I pause for a second, trying to decide whether to tell the whole story or just give the abbreviated version. To tell the whole story is too long. People who ask the question might have had other plans for their day and hadn't realized they were signing up for an hour-long story of someone's immigration journey, fraught with bribes and having "connections." But to shorten the tale is to cheat people of an important part of my culture in a critical time in the history of post-Soviet Ukraine: corruption in the Soviet bureaucracy.

Meeting Ruslana: Rob's Account

I was a student at Bethel Seminary preparing for the ministry. I was studying theology, philosophy, Greek, and Christian History, but

155

mostly thinking about girls. I had met two Ukrainian students at the seminary and had learned a lot about Ukraine. One of them, Yelena, said, "I know someone I think you would like to meet." She made arrangements for me to meet her friend, named Ruslana (?), and all three of us were going to go to a Halloween party. I waited the whole night for them to show up. I called her apartment, but Yelena didn't answer. We were supposed to meet at my apartment and then drive over together. Eventually, I drove half an hour to the party, and I asked around if they had shown up. My friends said, "Yes, they were here, and her friend was very nice." Since I had missed them I decided to drive all the way home again. I had given up on meeting this Ruslana.

When I was home, I got a call from Yelena. It was almost midnight, and she asked if I still wanted to meet her, and naturally, being a red-blooded male American, I said yes. They came over after midnight and I invited them in. Well, Ruslana walked in like she owned the place. She was not shy or withdrawn. She didn't even make eye contact with me when she walked in. She was looking around my apartment, wearing a black leather jacket and a white, fluffy sweater underneath and jeans. She carried herself like an Eastern Bloc Olympic gymnast with square shoulders and a determined stride. She had a very short, black, Juliette Binoche haircut and sparkling dark eyes. She reminded me a little of a younger Judy Garland ... and it was love at first sight. Well, for me, at least.

She and Yelena walked in and had a seat. I offered them a drink, and Ruslana asked for water. I don't think I was joking when I filled a tall glass up to the top with ice and added water. When I handed it to her she just looked at it and asked, "Would you like some water with your ice?" Actually, that is what she would say now, a nice American platitude. Back then, she would have said, "You gave me more ice than water. How am I supposed to drink this?"

I had just read Turgenev's Home of the Gentry, *and I showed her the several Russian books I had on the shelf, I learned very quickly that she was not Russian, that she was Ukrainian, so I had to figure all that out. What's the difference? When I was young, the Soviet Union was referred to as Russia, so I was brought up thinking of all those countries as Russia. I learned that there were fifteen different "sister" countries that made up the Soviet Union, kinda like how polygamists have "sister" wives. And it was not THE Ukraine, just Ukraine, and that to use THE in front of Ukraine was just an artifact of colonial and imperialist misunderstandings of the West and their decadent education system.*

So, as you can see, we hit it off right off the bat, or as Ruslana would say, "We hit the bat right off." We soon excused Yelena, who quickly took the hint and left. We would not see her again until she was a bridesmaid at our wedding. Ru, as I learned her family called her, and I spent hours more talking about Dostoevsky, what it feels like living in the breadbasket of Europe, and our faith in God.

Well, it turned out that we really made a connection. I loved her cute, lilting European accent and big, brown eyes, and she loved my sense of humor.

Meeting Rob: Ruslana's Account

It's our first date, November 3, 1997. Rob pulls up in his Chevy Corsica to my host parents' home. To be accurate, I don't notice the car. The only thing I notice is that I'm happy and I'm in love and I'm going on a date with him. We are driving to some people's house for dinner, and all I think about is him and I really want to get to know him, so I ask him about his family. What he says next causes me to think, "I can see spending the rest of my life with this guy. He makes me laugh." Laughter is important to me because humor is cultural, which means not everything that's funny to Ukrainians is funny to Americans and vice versa. But I get his humor and laugh until my sides hurt. He recites Neil Simon's *God's Favorite,*

> *"I'll tell you something ... There was a time in my life when the holes in my socks were so big, you could put them on from either end ... I grew up in a tenement in New York. My mother, my father and eleven kids in one and a half rooms. We had two beds and a cot, you had to take a number off the wall to go to sleep ..."*

He pulls off the best New York accent and does it so easily while driving us to somebody's house for dinner. I can barely chew gum and walk at the same time, but Rob can pull off an accent while driving in the dark.

Here's what you need to know about Rob. He has a degree from the University of Iowa (Go Hawks!) in theater, film, and communication, where Kurt Vonnegut taught writing classes. So, when he is reciting these lines, it is like sitting in a comedy theater and listening to a stand-up comedian. I laugh so hard, my mascara runs down my cheeks, my sides hurt, and I know I love him already. I tell him, "Stop, stop, stop. You are making me laugh so hard, you made me sick to my stomach." He replies, "Usually on a first date one of your goals is to avoid making your date sick to her stomach."

I feel at ease with Rob. I don't feel the need to impress him. I sit back with my head against the seat. He isn't arrogant like other guys I've met, but funny, smart, and he makes me feel good about myself just the way I am. I feel immediately comfortable around him. It's been twenty years, and I still laugh at those lines. If you haven't read *God's Favorite*, you should.

Rob continues explaining how we grew closer together.

> *I think we connected on three levels: culturally, philosophically, and spiritually. Even though we were from different, sometimes drastically different, cultures, our premarital counselor, Dr. Nils Friberg, told us that we were both culturally curious, and that we liked to learn about different cultures and people from other countries. What*

drew us together was an interest in the same things, like cultures, philosophy, or theology. We spent much of our time talking about our own observations about human nature, the Bible, new theories we've discovered and developed, and what we've read recently. And the way we connected the strongest was through our spiritual connection. Though (how do you say it, Ruthlana? Rush-lana?) Ruslana and I are from different cultures, we share a very similar outlook on life based on Scripture. We've both accepted Christ as our Savior, live for Him, pray as often as we can remember, and rely on God for our needs. We try not to worry about things, putting our trust in God.

One of the most interesting things about meeting people from other cultures, or living in another country, is to learn more about one's own culture. When I lived in Japan, I was able to understand my own culture better because I was able to view it in contrast to the Japanese culture. What I thought at first was weird was simply another, completely valid, way of doing things.

Even to this day, Ruslana and I analyze our own and each other's cultures. At our wedding reception, Ruslana said, "You can take the girl out of Ukraine, but you can't take Ukraine out of the girl." This is true. But what is even more interesting is trying to figure out if a person's own personality and characteristics are from their culture of origin, a family of origin, that person's own individual, quirky ways, or a combination of all three.

CHAPTER 12

"Rob, How Did You Like Ukraine?"

The KGB Lurks Around Every Corner

I t's March 1999 and Rob comes to Ukraine for the first time. We were married on August 15, 1998. But my parents couldn't come to our wedding because of the rigid visa laws on both sides. Ukraine gained its independence from the Soviet empire in 1991 but nothing really changed for a long time. A country does not break free from an oppressive colonizer and instantly becomes democratic and free. The remnant of corruption and law evasion were and still are holding the country in bondage. This is what Rob has to say about our trip. Some parts are embellished or exaggerated for humorous effect.

Ruslana was pretty nervous about our first trip to Ukraine together. We had only been married for nine months, and this was going to be the first time I met her parents. She was particularly concerned about us being robbed. I had traveled before to Spain, Mexico, Japan, the Philippines, and had lived in Los Angeles for six years, so I felt like I was a pretty seasoned traveler. What I lacked in street smarts I made up for in international experience. She made it very clear to me that the KGB lurked around every corner. She talked about how the Russian mafia would kill us in the streets and then steal all of our money. She told me not to let our baggage get more than a foot away from us because one guy would steal one bag at the airport or in the city and run away with it. And if I ran after him, another guy would steal our other bags while I was in a foot race to retrieve our first bag. She told me not to speak in English in bus terminals or airports because she knew they would hear my accent and think I was a rich American and charge us more for taxi rides or food. So I prepared for my trip to Ukraine without fear, but definitely with a question about what kind of country I was going to.

Ruslana has raised $7,000 from friends and family to give to her father to buy a tractor. I had purchased two money belts for us to wear on our flights from Chicago to Amsterdam, and then on to Kyiv. We split the money, so we each had $3,500 wrapped around our waists, plus our own traveling money. Also, many church friend Americans had given us money in envelopes, the total amount unknown to us, to pass along to Ukrainian friends and churches. So I honestly didn't know how much money I was carrying, but it was most likely well below the limit of $10,000 per person that travelers are allowed to take without declaring it. I was a little nervous having so much money on me, and especially in my briefcase. Well, wouldn't you know, as we were walking past security in Minneapolis on our way to the plane a federal agent pulls me aside, flashes his badge, and asks me how much money I'm taking with me. Usually, I'm traveling as a missionary, so I generally have less money on me than a junior high schooler, but this time I was loaded. I thought, "Oh my gosh, the mafia is already trying to rob me." When he asked how much money I had, I said about $7,000, which was actually twice as much as what I had because Ruslana had taken half the funds, but I thought of us as being together. He asked, "Where is the money?" I pulled him over to the side, lifted up my shirt and pulled on the belt, unzipped the top of it, and flashed the money. He said, "Okay," and I zipped up again and he let me go. I hurried to catch up with Ruslana and told her what happened. She said, "I told you so," and this encounter with the federal agent, unfortunately, served to further fuel her anxiety about being robbed.

I kept the money belt, which is more like a skinny fanny pack that you wear inside your shirt, on myself at all times during the flight. Flying through the night to Amsterdam, trying to catch some shut-eye, the belt slowly shimmied its way up my torso until it was wrapped around my chest. I felt like I was wearing a bra, which gave me a whole new perspective on the female demographic who need to wear those contraptions. I couldn't take it off because, you know, Russian mafia on the plane would kill and rob me, so I tried to slide it down before we arrived in the Netherlands.

Surviving the Airport in Kyiv

We departed from Amsterdam and flew into Kyiv, and as soon as the airplane hit the ground, I knew we weren't in Minnesota anymore. Everything had certainly taken a much darker turn. The airport in Borispol was less of an adventurer's layover and more of a quasi-military base where arriving foreigners were treated with suspicion, and rumors ran amok. The arrivals port was made of metal walls painted white with no stanchions to help arriving passengers to queue up. It was a free for all. Ruslana told me, "Don't worry about the airport Customs. You just walk through and they check your passport." "Okay," I said, "just don't leave me." "I will never leave you nor forsake you," Ruslana promised. Well, the first thing they did was split us up into two lines—one for Ukrainian nationals and one for the poor slobs who they could take advantage of.

Being one of those poor slobs, I stood in line hoping I wouldn't be frisked for my money or imprisoned for being a decadent American who was wearing a bra. No kidding, the security officers who checked everyone's passports looked like Soviet-era Red Army officers who wore military hats with a brim as wide around as a frisbee, and they didn't look happy. One American man, who looked like your typical New York City bourgeoisie, grabbed his wife by the hand and

took her in the opposite direction from the checkout, muttering something secretively about having to purchase health insurance to be
able to clear Customs. He took her behind us to other counters where
uniformed soldiers apparently sold health insurance policies. I don't
know if they offered Aflac. I heard people mutter about how this was
a communist country and that Americans couldn't get health care
without insurance. I had health insurance in America, plus I didn't
plan on visiting any post-Soviet-era hospitals on my stay. I stayed
in line, hoping to avoid having to buy health insurance. Things had
become very surreal very quickly. First of all, they demanded to know
how much money I had ... again. Then they made me make a list of
all the jewelry I had carried with me. Why in the world did they need
to know how much jewelry I had? When I arrived at Narita airport in
Japan years ago they didn't ask, "How much money do you have?"
When I landed in Paris they didn't ask, "What jewelry are you bringing in?" Again, I thought, they're asking me how much money I have
so they can find fault with me and make me pay bribes or some bogus
fees or tax. I didn't know what was going on. They asked me for my
purpose there. I said to see family. The commissar was sitting behind
bulletproof glass about four feet higher than me, so I looked up at
him on his throne and wondered if I would ever see my wife again.
He looked at my passport, then at me, and then at the passport again,
as if I might be the first seminary student from Bethel Seminary who
was a drug mule smuggling lutefisk from Minneapolis to Kyiv. He
finally released me, saying I had three days to register with the local
militsia, or military police when I finally arrived at my destination. If
I arrive at my destination.

By the time I survived this process, Ruslana was already in Young
Pioneer mode: ready, always ready. She got through her line quicker,
had picked up two carts for us to put our luggage on, and was
hurrying to the exit. There was something I learned about Ruslana
at that time. She had been raised in the Soviet Union, and in order

to survive their system, she had learned to cut corners, hustle, use whatever leverage you needed to succeed, and work the system. She was suddenly a different person. The Ruslana I knew in America was this laid-back, easy-going girlfriend and newlywed, who went with me to see movies and go shopping at The Gap. Once we hit Customs, she shifted into Ukraine-mode. She was large and in charge. She was suddenly in her element and started implementing the survival skills she had learned after years in the big city.

The exit was another security stop in which they would go through all my bags to see what I had brought. Now, I was standing behind my cart with my luggage, just like an American would stand behind their shopping cart at your friendly neighborhood Target. So, I politely guided my cart to one of the amassed lines to exit the arrivals section. One young Ukrainian man pulled up his cart next to me and saw a foot of space between myself and the woman in front of me. He quickly pushed his way in front of me, completely blocking my way, and I thought, "My, isn't that rude." He didn't follow the unspoken rule of American shopping in which we kindly guide our carts to the checkout lane, gently motion for other shoppers to go in front of us if they don't have much to buy, and get in a nice orderly line where we check email, read the cover of scandalous magazines we would never think of buying, and fight the temptation to buy a candy bar. This gentleman obviously wasn't familiar with this rule. Neither was the next guy who cut in line. And the next guy who budged in line. I quickly learned that I wasn't going to get anywhere unless I got with the program. I saw Ruslana had already gotten through the line; apparently, she wasn't familiar with the unwritten rules of line-waiting either. Now, I had been a linebacker, a wrestler, and a shot-putter, so I was no shrinking violet, but generally, I didn't accost people to get into a line. But dire times call for dire measures. I had to push my cart right up behind the last guy who cut in front of me, and, of course, another rough guy tried to weasel his way in. I put my shoulder up against him to drive him off, but he was determined to force his way in. I had finally lost my patience with this. I yelled at him so everybody around me could hear, "What do we have to do, get in a fight about this?" He looked at me, saw I was serious, and he got behind me. I had quickly acclimated to the culture.

They looked in my bags, in which I mostly had gifts for our family and envelopes in my briefcase. The arrivals greeting area was a madhouse. In America there were, at that time, little ropes which greeters stood behind, holding cards with travelers' names on them. In Kyiv, there were no little ropes to hold the masses back. People just walked into the processing area looking for arriving family members, and the crowd outside was loud and pushy, like a mob at a rock concert. A man came up to me and kissed me on both my cheeks, his five o'clock shadow chafing my skin. It was my father-in-law, Anatoliy. He helped Ruslana with her bags as I kept an eye out for KGB, gypsies, tramps, and thieves.

On our way to their house, a four-hour drive through some of the roughest roads this side of northern Wisconsin, Ruslana's dad stopped to buy bread. I learned that it was common to stop by the side of the city streets to pick up freshly baked bread. He picked up two unsliced loaves which were as dark as pumpernickel and big as a football, and threw them, with no bags or wrappers, into the back window of the 20-year-old Volkswagen Golf. I just looked at the loaves sitting in the dirty back window ledge and thought, "I think he may be breaking some local, state, and federal laws concerning food handling and safety. He must not have heard of the Food Safety Modernization Act created to reduce the risk of foodborne illness." Well, neither had the rest of the country.

I soon discovered that food handling was very different in Ukraine. There weren't your typical grocery stores like Cubs, Krogers, or Jewels. Many people raised their own pigs, chickens, geese, and turkeys. They grew their own gardens of potatoes, cabbage, and other greens. Many people who lived in Ruslana's village raised or cultivated their own food. They did have small grocers, like a small 7-11 that sells selected groceries.

"Ya ne znayu."

One of the things Ruslana learned she had to do while in Ukraine was to get a new passport. The passport she was traveling on in 1999 was an old passport issued by the Soviet Union, and she had to get a new passport issued by the country of Ukraine, not the Ukrainian Soviet Socialist Republic. While visiting her hometown of Buzhanka, I knew the one thing I would not do was to go to the nearest militsia government building to register. Well, Ruslana had to go to the militsia to get a new passport.

I was not really comfortable being there. I was wearing my bright yellow North Face jacket while everybody else had dark gray or black leather jackets. It took forever for the classic bureaucratic paperwork, with me sitting in the hallway waiting for them to process her request. So many people came up to me and asked me something in Ukrainian about the large office I was waiting outside of. I answered with the only Russian I knew, "Ya ne znayu," which means "I don't know." They would look at me like I was nuts or stupid. I think they were asking me, "Are you waiting for a new document?" and I was answering, "I don't know." "Are you waiting for your family?" "I don't know." I didn't want to speak in English so they could get the hint that I was a foreigner because I didn't want to have to register with the militsia, because I didn't know what that meant. Was I going to be drafted? Were they going to interrogate me? Also, it had been made clear to me that if I spoke in English I would be robbed and murdered, so I just continued to tell anyone who would ask that I didn't know anything. I felt like Sgt. Schultz repeating, "Nothing. I know nothing."

By the end of our stay, I was sick of not being able to explore the country I was visiting. After a week of being kept indoors and not visiting cities or going shopping, I would have welcomed the KGB stealing my money and the mafia kidnapping me. When I was at a bus station I wanted to ask a saleswoman for a Twix.

Ruslana said, "No! What would you ask her?" I said, "Ya hochu Twix." I want a Twix. "No, you can't say that. We would say Tveex. Someone might rob you."

At that point, I didn't care if they did rob me. I went up to the woman who was selling candy bars out of a cardboard box near the ticket window and said "I want Tveex, please," and she sold me one. I am pleased to report that I survived that experience.

Ruslana's Take On It

To be fair, many of Rob's observations are valid. Those things did happen. Bear in mind, this was in 1999. The Ukrainian government was still a shadow of the Soviet government and things hadn't changed that much yet. If you ask me, even today, things haven't changed much at some levels. Yes, the Boryspil airport has been remodeled with a fancy duty-free section, a coffee bar, and a second floor for international arrivals. The security guards aren't looking to solicit bribes from you. And there is even a poster hanging that says, "If you see corruption, report it." However, at the time of our earlier travels, there was overt corruption in the government and government officials looked for every opportunity to find a reason for being paid a bribe. Due to the fact that government officials had unrestrained authority over people with no fear of repercussions, they would take advantage of any opportunity to solicit bribes or favors for their services.

In terms of the fear of us being robbed, it was more the fear of being overcharged as an American. That was a true fact.

CHAPTER 13

"What's it Like Being Married
to an American?"

Thereisno word for privacy in the Ukrainian Language.

"Ru, can you close the door, please?"

"Ru, you forgot to close the door again."

"Ru, this door lock will not lock. I need to close the door."

In my house in Ukraine, we have bedroom and bathroom doors, but I think they are more decorative than functional (especially the bathroom). In Rob's family, doors exist to help people have their privacy. In Ukraine, we don't even have a word for privacy. Interesting thing, language, isn't it? Language is a repository of a culture. If a culture doesn't have a concept, why have a word to hold a concept that doesn't exist?

In my family, people change clothes in front of each other, walk around in their underwear, and sometimes don't use locks on bathroom doors. Toddlers swim in the river and run around on the beach naked. That's how Julian is potty-trained, by peeing on pebbles on the shore of the Black Sea in the Crimea. There are no obstacles caused by wearing underwear, and the pebbles are a lot more fun to pee on than a plastic potty. The public doesn't stare because it's an accepted practice. You would not see this happening at a community beach in Minnesota or Wisconsin. I remember being kicked out of a community pool when Julian was wearing underwear and not a diaper as a

My parents and Julian in the Crimea, Summer 2004.

baby. Of course, I entirely agree with and respect U.S. laws when it comes to these issues now, especially when it comes to public pools.

Another influence on the formation of my concept of privacy comes from attending schools in Ukraine in the 1980s that didn't have doors on their bathroom stalls. I'm in seventh grade. It's January, about 15 below zero. To go to the bathroom, we have to go outside. There is a small outdoor bathroom building built of brick with stalls made out of cement, like a bathroom pavilion at a public park in America. But it doesn't have toilet seats to sit on, just a hole in the cement floor for me to squat over. The stench from those holes is so bad, it burns my eyes, and the pungent smell follows me on my clothes all the way to my next algebra class.

Since there are no doors on the stalls, I just walk by it to see with the corner of my eye if it's occupied. I bring my own "toilet paper," which is the communist newspaper Pravda (which means truth), and the truth is that this is probably the best use for that paper. When Americans start coming and conducting Vacation Bible Schools on the school grounds, the first item on their agenda is to finance new indoor toilets. I don't reap the benefits of those because it happens after my days.

When I travel across America by car, I am amazed at the notion of rest areas. I've lived here since 1995 and I still don't take them for granted.

All of us together. Dad, mom, Rob in the center. Myself, Bogdan, Alla, and baba Manya. March 1999.

They literally put a smile on my face. I wonder if they are invented by the Democrats—such a people-focused service! No strings attached. Rest areas are completely free of charge. You are not required to buy anything there, but there are vending machines for your convenience if you want a sugar or protein kick for the rest of your trip. They have picnic tables for summer use. There are garbage and recycling bins to clean your car out during your road trip. There is plenty of parking and shade where you can take a nap and shake off your drowsiness. The bathrooms and toilets are always free. And last but not least, it has toilet paper, tons of it. And you don't have to pay per inch.

In Ukraine, our rest areas are bushes and trees along the side of the road. I'll never forget this story when American missionaries were picked up by bus in Kyiv and they asked the bus driver to stop at the next bathroom, he immediately slammed on his brakes, opened the door, and yelled to everyone, "Anybody needs toilet?" The first timers were like, "Where exactly is the bathroom here?" Those with more experience showed them which bushes to pick to squat behind and how to avoid thistles and stinging nettles.

When Rob comes to Ukraine with me for the first time, he tries really hard to enjoy himself and embrace this new culture. There are fun times and challenging times. Privacy is in the challenging category. My parents have a custom of offering their own bedroom for the comfort of special guests. They sleep in the other room on the couch on the veranda. My parents' bedroom is one of two rooms in the house that has a door, but it's a decorative or hypothetical door. Growing up, it's never closed for privacy. There are curtains hanging on the doorframe. My parents just draw the curtains over and that's enough. I think the only reason we have doors in our house is so that we have a place to hang our bath towels for drying. Rob, to ensure privacy for himself, tries to close our parents' bedroom door when going to bed or changing in the morning. The handle doesn't function well and easily breaks. So, every time we visit my family, my father ends up having to fix the bedroom door.

So, how does privacy play out in a cross-cultural marriage in the U.S. where doors have locks on them? In America, whenever Rob takes a shower in the bathroom, which is in our bedroom, he always closes the bedroom and the bathroom door. I always leave it open and don't even notice. And this has been going on for 20 years. Old habits die hard. I wonder if they have marriage therapists who specialize in cross-cultural concepts of privacy.

Honey, What I Think You're You Trying to Say is ...

Rob and I always enjoy laughing together (remember from the introduction, that's why I married him). Some of the time I find that Rob is laughing at me, not with me. But he does so in love. We have developed a tradition in our home of Rob trying to figure out what I'm trying to say. When editing this book, half the time Rob would say, "Honey, what are you trying to say here?" For example, when I say, "I flew off the roof," Rob thinks for a second and I can see the linguistic gears in his head turning. I can almost hear the grinding sound of the gears, trying to figure out what I'm trying to say. Then he says, "I think what you are trying to say is 'you flew off the handle' or 'you hit the roof' but you merged them together." I have many more sayings like this. The other morning it was negative 11 degrees Fahrenheit. I told Julian to preheat his car before he left for school. Rob asked, "To 450 degrees?"

You see, the English language is my main language now, but it's actually easier for me to speak in the academic register. You'd think speaking colloquially would be easier and specialized registers would be harder. But that's not how it works. Colloquial and idiomatic ways of speaking are harder as I explained in the chapter on communication faux pas. But I get excited every time I appropriately use colloquial phrasing in context because it helps me sound like I belong. And belonging is very important to me, especially when I try to fit in with my U.S. church friends or coffee buddies, not just my academic community friends.

One example of excitement is when I say to the boys who love a good burger, "Let's go check out this new burger joint." instead of saying "Shall we go eat at the new hamburger restaurant?" Rob later explains that "checking out a new burger joint" sounds like something out of a movie set in New Jersey in the '50s. I learn that my use of slang or colloquialisms is never natural. It feels awkward and pretentious, but I enjoy taking risks, even if it reminds natives that I'm not from here.

Germs Are an Invention of the West

"Honey, why did you leave the milk out?"

"Sorry, I didn't realize it. I'll put it away."

One of our cross-cultural clashes in marriage "germinate" in a discussion about germs, and the concept of what is considered clean and dirty. Rob grew up in the suburbs where he wasn't allowed to leave milk out on the counter because it would go sour. I grew up on a farm.

As a child my mom asks me to go to my grandfather's house, about a two-mile walk, to bring a gallon of fresh cow milk. I love visiting my grandparents. On my way there, I snack on cherries, mulberries, apricots, and apples, picking them off the neighbors' trees. The streets are lined with cherry trees. The cherries have this thin layer of dust on them, but we just rub them on our shirts and eat them right there on the gravel road. Don't worry, this was before 1986 and the Chernobyl disaster, so the dust isn't radioactive yet. I never get sick from eating fruit right off the trees. We eat until our bellies are full. The neighbors are kind and don't scold us for eating off of their trees. How much can a kid eat? Five cherries per tree on each trip?

Once at my grandparents', I get the gallon glass jar of milk, spend an hour talking, and then take another hour to get back home. There is no refrigerated cooler to transport the milk. I just carry it in a sturdy bag. I bring it home and leave it on the kitchen table for everyone to enjoy. Mom uses it for cooking. Dad drinks straight out of a jar. We never get sick from unrefrigerated milk. In fact, it's still warm because it's straight from the cow's teat. If you want to sour milk for making *vareniki* (aka pierogi) or pancakes, then you leave the milk on the table for it to go sour naturally.

We also have a different way of doing things in terms of cooking. On weekends, we make food midmorning and then leave it on the stove to eat the rest of the day. I remember bringing Tupperware containers to Ukraine to save leftovers to put them in the fridge, but Mom never used them. She put them away with other fancy dishes that are used once a year for special guests. Leftovers are not a thing. You'd eat some leftovers, but not all of them, because, as mom said, "Pigs have to eat something too." We use the leftovers to feed the dog, Barsik; the cat, Murchik; and drizzle them over the pig feed to make it tastier for the pigs.

So, when I am first married to Rob, we have arguments about germs. Rob always tells me about *e coli* and *salmonella*, and all I remember is my childhood and how we ate raw *salo* and drank raw eggs (*gogol mogol*) and never got sick. We butcher a pig and have the meat lie there on the table with the pig head looking at us until all the meat is sorted, canned, frozen, or cooked. That's why we butcher pigs in the winter to take advantage of the natural refrigeration.

Now, in our marriage, I don't leave the pig head out on the kitchen counter forever, and I don't leave milk sitting out in a jar all day to wait until it turns sour. I follow common sense safety rules, but I still catch myself not following them to the same degree that Rob's family did. For example, I definitely wash fruit in the U.S. because it's covered either in wax or pesticides. But I also leave pancakes sitting out on a plate all day after breakfast for kids to snack on.

Go Meta or Go Home

So, how do I conclude the chapter on cross-cultural marital arguments? When we are first married, we just argue about these "health issues" and I try to prove with my loud voice that I am right. Rob responds with his scientific knowledge and describes to me how germs are formed on food. Or he just walks away and will bring up the subject about 24 hours later when I'm being more reasonable and cool off a bit. By that time, I don't remember it anymore and it's water under the bridge.

My honey Rob and I, Fall 2018.

But then we learn how to look at it as differences that stem from our families of origin and our cultures. In marriage, two people come together and bring with them the practices and habits of their families of origin, whether intentionally or unintentionally, consciously or unconsciously. It is better when in a marital relationship to be aware of these cultural differences and approach these clashes with this in mind, even if you are from the same country. Also, be ready to make some major sacrifices and compromises to make your marriage work. I finally gave in that the toilet paper should hang over, not under. But we couldn't resolve the toothpaste argument because I always squeezed it from the top, so I ended up buying my own. As I write this, I realize that my parents used the same tube of toothpaste (and sometimes we used baking soda), and they never discussed which end to squeeze it from because they had more important issues to discuss. As for the toilet paper, well, if it's the newspaper, and not the roll, then the argument is solved by itself. Just rip it and pierce it through a nail.

We all bring with us unique practices, such as how we celebrate birthdays, how we handle privacy, how we communicate, and how we resolve conflict. They are not right or wrong ways of doing things; they are just different. So, "going meta" means rising above those differences and seeing the bigger picture that cross-cultural marriage is about cultural explorations. Instead of allowing these differences to saddle a relationship with conflict and arguments, a multicultural couple can learn to understand these differences, enjoy each other's company, and use them as opportunities for cross-cultural conversations (except for those times we drive each other mad.)

CHAPTER 14:

"What Was It Like to Become an American Citizen?"

From "Alien" to Naturalized Citizen

I t's June 21, 2006. I'm in a Federal courtroom, in Saint Paul, Minnesota. I stand proud and tall, wearing my best-looking red suit along with other people from "every tribe, tongue, and nation," every one of us eager to take that final step on our journey to citizenship by taking an oath of allegiance to the United States. One small step for each of us, but one giant leap toward becoming a naturalized citizen.

Before becoming naturalized, we are unnatural, I guess. Isn't there a song that goes, "We are pilgrims, we are aliens, we are not of this world."?

Before this, I was an alien visitor on an exchange teacher's J1-visa, which allowed

Ron, Caryl, myself, and the judge at my citizenship ceremony, July 2006.

me to gain experience in being a teacher in the United States. As a visitor, one is categorized as a "nonresident alien." According to Homeland Security, to be promoted to the status of "resident alien" and to be given a green card, I have to fill out many applications and go to interviews. Over the years, I have discovered a double standard in the U.S. government. The immigration office is not in a hurry to give immigrants a status, but the IRS office actually creates various ways to ensure that, whether you are here legally or not, you still have a way to pay taxes.

Now I think I understand why we were called aliens before citizens. The first five years in America, I definitely feel like an alien on a different planet. Years later, it makes sense why one of the requirements in the process of becoming a citizen is to have lived in the U.S. for at least five years. The feeling of being an alien begins to wear off by the end of year five. It took me five years just to get used to eating casseroles and not saying "let me through" in a grocery store. Likewise, people are beginning to get used to my spaceship, green skin, and antennae sticking out of the top of my head.

Let's talk about the descriptors the government created to label us, the immigrants: alien, resident alien, and naturalized citizens. There's definitely a progression there from less human to more human. When I say, "the government," I don't mean some abstract entity, but human beings like you and me. Someone, who probably never experienced what it feels like to be an immigrant, after a brief discussion on some Wednesday afternoon, decided that a suitable term to use to describe us would be alien. The reasoning probably was, "Well, they aren't residents or citizens yet and they don't have a status yet, so let's call them aliens." I realize that other countries use terms like "foreigner" to refer to people who are visiting their countries. But think about the meaning that the term alien connotes. Just doing a quick look in Google search, the Wikipedia description is:

> "In law, an alien is a person who is not a citizen or national of a given country, though definitions and terminology differ to some degree depending on the continent or region of the world. The term "alien"

basically means a foreign national. ... The term "alien" is derived from the Latin *alienus*, meaning *stranger, foreigner, belonging somewhere else.*"

We, the immigrants, wish to thank those people who welcomed us into their borders from our distant planets and labeled us aliens. What a warm and fuzzy way to help us fit right in. Welcome to the U.S. of A.!

Of course, we do need a legal term to refer to immigrants who aren't naturalized yet. But what if we look to more humane names for guests and residents and citizens? Otherwise, every time I hear the term alien, I have the image of the *Mars Attacks* aliens saying "Ack, ack-ack, ack-ack-ack." I wonder if that's what Ukrainian or Telugu or Somali sounds like to the monolingual English-speaking ear.

The same can be said about the term "naturalized." First, we are called aliens. And in addition, we are un-naturalized aliens. What does that tell you about how the immigration office categorizes us and dehumanizes us in the process?

Becoming a U.S. Citizen in Five Easy Steps

The road to citizenship is not an easy one. Most Americans probably think that foreigners come here on a visa, apply for and get a green card, apply for citizenship after five years, take an oath of allegiance to the U.S., and voilà, you're an American citizen. Just five easy steps. The process is actually fraught with so many challenges that it often takes a miracle, a fake marriage, and $10,000 in lawyers' fees to become a citizen. In my case, it was a combination of a miracle and a marriage, but not a fake one.

It's 1997, the year Princess Diana dies in a car crash, *The Lion King* hits Broadway, *The X-Files* is a hit on TV, and I am an ESL teacher at Taylors Falls Elementary School. My employer is a public school district where I teach English as a Second Language. My boss is a very supportive principal who goes above and beyond to help me gather all the paperwork I need to document that I qualify for an H-1B worker visa. The H-1B is a visa that allows companies in the United States to temporarily employ foreign workers in occupations that require the theoretical and practical application of a body of highly specialized knowledge and a bachelor's degree (or its equivalent) or higher in the specific specialty.

Since starting at the school, I have had a work authorization permit that is about to expire. To extend my work permit I have to apply for a different visa since the extension to my current permit is not an option. I have a three-inch-thick stack of papers to prove how excruciatingly painful the process is. To qualify for the H-1B visa, one of the many things my employer has to prove is that there is nobody available to fill the position that I hold. My principal has proof of many posted advertisements for this position that no one wants to fill. Taylors Falls is a rural community 50 miles outside of the Twin Cities, which makes the process of finding a teacher to fill that position very challenging. I don't mind driving an hour and ten minutes each way for five years because I love my work.

However, the immigration office reviewing my case does not find the evidence convincing enough, or maybe they woke up on the wrong side of the bed that day, but I all I know is that I am not having any luck in obtaining the desired visa. If I don't have the visa, I am not able to continue working and will have to return to my country.

I meet Rob in October 1997. We date for nine months, fall in love, and marry on August 15, 1998. Now that I am married to an American, I am able to apply for a green card, which is a residency card and will allow me to apply for citizenship in five years. Ironically, I finally receive my H-1B application approval in the mail upon return from our honeymoon. This visa is now rendered essentially moot because I am on my path toward residency as the wife of an American citizen.

To apply for a permanent resident status, we go to the Immigration and

Naturalization Services Office (INS, before it was very appropriately re-named as ICE) and bring evidence that our marriage is real. We show the official pictures from our wedding ceremony, which was the most wonderful celebration on earth. The missions team from Ham Lake Church, who usually travel to Ukraine to host an Adventure Camp for the children in my home village of Buzhanka, couldn't make it that summer. So they offered to host our wedding and provide the church, meeting hall, and reception meal. We had 250 people with pastor Fred Tuma and Sandy McMacken as the officiants. My friend did my flowers using blue and yellow Ukrainian colors. The dinner was ham sandwiches with *korovai,* a traditional Ukrainian wedding bread. After seeing the photos of such a wonderful celebration with the authentic Ukrainian bread, how could the immigration officers doubt that our marriage was real?

Proving the validity of our marriage is easy because we have nothing to hide, but the officer interrogates us in different rooms. "Interrogates" is a strong word. It's more like a conversation, but I am nervous, because it takes place in an INS office, not in our living room, and the stakes are high since the future of our life together depends on the outcome of this conversation.

Five years later, taking the citizenship test makes me uneasy. My future depends on whether I know the answers about the American Revolution or the three branches of the government or criteria for the privilege to vote. The INS agent smiles, and his smile takes me back to the Ukrainian government offices where the government officials don't smile at all. Their job is to make you feel inferior by exerting their bureaucratic power over you.

I'm relieved not to be in a Ukrainian government office, but I am nervous because I am not sure if I know American history that well. Is the father of our country George Washington or Abraham Lincoln? I say George Washington and get a positive affirmation that I got it right. He is asking me questions about the American Revolution and basic civics. I don't remember the exact questions, but I remember getting them right. There are no multiple-choice questions about the internment of the Japanese or the forced resettlement of the Native Americans.

I don't remember the written exam to test my English, but I'm glad they don't test me on the use of the article "the" and appropriate questions to use to engage in small talk.

My three passports spanning from my Soviet to American citizenships.

Finally, after all of those steps, I become a citizen. It is in 2006, a year after Nicky, my second child, is born. It's strange to think a non-citizen gave birth to two citizens.

I will never forget the citizenship ceremony. It is an important day. I am taking an oath of allegiance to my new country. At the same time, I am firmly holding on to the Ukrainian flag, standing tall and proud of my ethnicity and my identity. It is an emotional decision and I know what it feels like to pledge allegiance to one country and holding on to the country of your birthplace, where *moya pupovina zahovana,* my umbilical cord is buried.

CHAPTER 15

"Do Your Kids Speak Ukrainian?"

Growing up with Linguistic Insecurity

I wake up from a nightmare that reveals my biggest fear and reality—my children are not bilingual. In this dream I am answering the ubiquitous question, "Are your children bilingual?" or "Do they speak Ukrainian?" I respond with, "They understand some Ukrainian and speak a few words." Julian interrupts me proudly and says very fluently, "*Я очень люблю говорить по-русски,*" which means, "I love speaking Russian." I am proud that he is taking a world language, but disappointed at the same time that it's not Ukrainian. Even in my dreams, I worry about my children's bilingualism and set out to describe the challenges and complexities of raising bilingual children.

When the kids are born, I talk to them in Ukrainian off and on. Because Rob speaks English with a few memorized phrases in Russian and Ukrainian (and often it's both languages in one sentence), when I talk to the boys in Ukrainian and then switch to talk to Rob, my brain does a switcharoo and I either say something to him in Ukrainian or back to the babies in English. There is no wonder that bilingualism protects against Alzheimer's because your brain is doing acrobatic back flips all the time. It's like an intense cardio workout going back and forth with two languages.

The success of the "one parent - one language" method depends on many factors. As a person who grew up on both sides of the Soviet empire, before

183

and after the regime's collapse, I am not confident in using Ukrainian because we grew up with the stigma that Ukrainian was a language of the lower class. In my childhood, Russian is the cool language. Russian is the language of the city. I am from the *selo*, a village kid.

If you grew up in the United States, and someone mentions the Village People, it conjures up images of a cop, a construction worker, and other characters singing the songs "YMCA" and "Macho Man." In Ukraine, the village people, *selyany,* is a derogatory term, describing someone from a lower class. Russian is the language of TV, the language of prestige, knowledge, and intelligence. Ukrainian is the language for the village folks, for planting and harvesting potatoes, for working in the sugar beet factory, for swimming in the river, and for living in a single-family home with a vegetable garden versus living in a *квартира (kvartira)*, an apartment. I don't want to be from the *selo*. Even when playing with dolls, our dolls live in this make-believe world where everyone is cool and everyone spoke Russian and everyone lived in a *kvartira* and no one was growing potatoes.

As a child, I switch to Russian when traveling to a city. One day we take the bus to Cherkassy, a city two hours away by car and three and a half hours away by bus. My dad and I go by bus. I am wearing a beautiful long, narrow dress my sister sewed for me. The aisle on the bus is full of passengers' bags and navigating my way through them in a long, narrow dress that wraps around my legs is hard. I trip over a bag and have to say "I'm sorry," which is *Eezvenitye* in Russian and not *Vybachte* in Ukranian.

Try to wrap your head around this. I live in a country where the official language is Ukrainian, but it holds a minority language status. If you are a native speaker of standard American English, it may be more difficult to put yourself in my shoes because English is not only the de facto official language of the U.S., but is THE international language for global communication. Consequently, no matter where you go in the world, you are already positioned as a person with privilege because you speak English. You don't have to worry about opening your mouth and sounding like you are from a *selo*.

The status of Ukrainian reminds me of the status of many rural dialects of English, like Appalachian English, as one example. The only difference is that Ukrainian was the official language of my country, not a regional dialect, and yet it held the status of a rural regional dialect wrongfully and discriminately associated with the lower class.

Having grown up with a linguistic insecurity, it catches up with me later in life when I am trying to teach my children Ukrainian. The question becomes, why should I teach Russian if it's not my language? It wins the popularity contest but loses the family connection contest. But teaching Ukrainian brings another question, which Ukrainian should I speak to the kids? Julian was born in 2001. Ukraine is now independent. The status of the Ukrainian language is slowly rising and my parents speak Ukrainian. Should I teach my kids the *літературну* or literary standard Ukrainian or the colloquial Ukrainian that I speak with my parents? The Standard Ukrainian is for newscasters and formal settings. When you use that dialect with your loved ones, you sound distant, almost standoffish, and not familial. Colloquial Ukrainian is too casual. It is only an oral dialect. Whenever we write, we switch to Standard Ukrainian. The colloquial Ukrainian I grew up speaking was called *суржик*, *Surzhik*, which is a word that means a mixture of wheat and rye. In this case, it's the result of Russian influences on the Ukrainian language.

Surzhik is the dialect of my dear grandma, Baba Manya. She is my mom's mom and is a gentle, soft-spoken woman who teaches me the value of slowing down when sipping your tea. Potatoes call to be weeded or harvested or sorted, but she doesn't care. She always makes time for tea. I learn this from her. Her tea rituals are simple. There are no fancy hats involved, which I will discover is the typical association with tea in the U.S. There are no delicate china cups and saucers with golden rims. Baba Manya just uses a mug that Americans brought over from Minnesota. In the U.S., mugs are abundant because they are used in marketing. In Ukraine, I grow up with small teacups, but we really like the large American mugs because they hold more tea and allow for longer conversations.

This particular mug is green with the words Ham Lake Baptist Church printed in gold paint. You couldn't see tea stains as easily on dark green porcelain. But Baba Manya taught me how to use baking soda to clean the stains. It's a Ukrainian life hack I bring to Minnesota and get raving reviews on this amazing "discovery."

We always have tea with *kanfeta,* which is *Surzhik* for *tsukerka* in standard Ukrainian or candy. My grandma's favorite *kanfeta* is *batonchik,* a fake chocolate candy in a cylindrical shape. We also eat oatmeal cookies. We don't bake them ourselves. We just buy them at the store. Before pouring tea, Baba Manya teaches me to warm up the cup by swishing boiling water in it. Baba Manya always drinks it piping hot, without burning her lips or the roof of her mouth. I eventually learn that skill from her and it serves me well to this day. Like her, I can't drink lukewarm tea or tea made with microwaved water. This is one area where I haven't budged in accommodating new ways to become more American. I'm definitely very Ukrainian in my tea drinking practices. They are sacred to me. They remind me of where I come from and who my people are.

Now in America, I lose my language all over again. The first years of my life I was losing it to Russian. This time I am losing Ukrainian to English. I don't have Ukrainian words for "identity" or "linguistic insecurity" or "bilingualism," I only have them in English. I find that I speak to myself in English. I don't have Ukrainian words when I read books of my profession, like Halliday's *Learning to Mean.*

But when I pray for my parents, I pray in Ukrainian. It's the only time I pray in Ukrainian. When I pray for my children and for my friends, I pray in English. I realize that even my prayer time in Ukrainian shrinks because I don't pray for my mom anymore. She is no longer among the living who need prayer. She has passed on. I try to extend my prayer time for my dad in Ukrainian, so I have that link to my language and my earthly *tato,* dad, and my loving Heavenly Father, through prayer. I fear that one day my use of Ukrainian will shrink to nothing.

Many days I catch myself speaking in Ukrainian when no one is around. In fact, most of the time, I don't have anyone around to speak Ukrainian with. I explain later in the book the struggle of raising children bilingually. Do you remember the last time you didn't have anyone to speak to in your native language? Do you know what that hunger feels like? You turn the TV on, and your language is not there. You go outside and talk to your neighbor, and your language isn't there. You look for it everywhere, but it's hard to find.

I find it in Skype conversations with my dad. I found it in my mother's voice when she was still living. I find it in my own thoughts, but it's very, very quiet … or it sounds translated from English and not natural. Every once in a while I have to meet with other Ukrainians just to get the taste back in my mouth. I'm very happy to have a family that speaks in English, and my whole profession is the study of teaching English to non-native speakers. But every once in a while, it's good to speak my mother tongue, if only to myself.

As an immigrant who has been living for two and a half decades of my adult life in the U.S., I am losing touch with the more recent developments in Ukraine. I can't answer questions about why Ukrainians have elected a comedian for a president. I feel like I'm no longer on the inside. I can't follow the narrative. I'm not in the narrative. I cry during the brutal days of the Maidan Revolution. I miss being in a community with other Ukrainians to feel and cry together. I miss out because I am not there during the Maidan Revolution of Dignity.

I am not there during the resurgence of the Ukrainian identity. I am not there to walk through the streets in my *vyshyvanka* (embroidered shirt) on May

187

16th to celebrate the National and International Vyshyvanka Day, which is a day when everyone—children, men, and women—show off their Ukrainian pride by wearing an embroidered shirt. I join my Ukrainian compatriots by wearing a shirt to work, but no one else is wearing one. I realize again that I carry Ukraine inside me by myself, but like many other diasporic Ukrainians who are scattered all over the world, we are Ukraine outside of Ukraine. I use social media to connect with Ukrainians worldwide to feel like I still belong and I can somehow to contribute to the Ukrainian community. The Ukrainian spirit of dignity created by the people whose protests brought down president Yanukovych reignites my Ukraine-ness inside me and I feel it's alive again. But then the flame grows smaller and my American-ness takes over. There is an ebb and flow to my ethnic self.

Language Policing

After decades of Russian linguistic imperialism, it is only natural for Ukraine to take steps to cleanse their language from foreign influences. The efforts to eliminate the *Surzhik* dialect are explained by the many attempts to deprive Ukrainians of their own language during the Stalin era. To deprive people of their own language means to deny them their own identity. Current efforts of language policing address all linguistic elements, from pronunciation to stress on syllables to vocabulary that will, supposedly, lead to the successful eradication of such "unclean" dialects as *Surzhik*.

I heard a linguist on a Ukrainian talk show say that because of language policing, some people are nervous about speaking standard Ukrainian because they are afraid that after years of speaking Russian will mean their Ukrainian is not "clean enough." In the 1980s, speaking Ukrainian isn't prestigious enough, and in the 2010s, the fear comes from not speaking it well enough. But other people, especially the older generation, continue to speak *Surzhik* to get all sorts of business done, from shopping to going to the bank to yelling at their neighbors. I can see my neighbor Halya yelling to her neighbor, "Get your chickens off my property!" speaking perfect *Surzhik.* As if an 80-year-old Ukrainian *selyanka* village woman is going to clean up her language from Russian influence and stop speaking *Surzhik* and switch to Standard Ukrainian in the middle of her yelling! The only cleaning it might need is the swear words, but that would cut her vocabulary in half. But to the purists, I say this: there is a place for standard Ukrainian and there is no need to eradicate dialects, no matter how politicized their origins may be.

The kids are young and I speak *Surzhik* with our boys. I say the word *kanfeta* instead of *tsukerka* for candy because my grandma used that word and it sounded creamy and smooth like good chocolate *kanfeta. Tsukerka* is too "cleaned up" and not quite familial. On one hand, *kanfeta* sounds wrong and I hear the judgment of purist Ukrainians in the back of my head. I switch to *tsukerka* in Standard Ukrainian, and it is too formal, too correct, like on TV.

As I decide that I am going to teach my children Ukrainian and not Russian, another issue arises: there are not enough Ukrainian speakers around. Julian is three and a half when I take him to Ukraine for the third time. As he spends some time with my parents and hears Ukrainian in the community, he says, "Mom, the whole country speaks your language." Before this, he only heard Ukrainian from me. Back in Minnesota, all my Ukrainian friends speak Russian except for one, and we live far apart, seeing each once a month at the most.

Of course, I can take them to a Saturday Ukrainian language school in Minneapolis, but the rumors are that community speaks and teaches the North American Ukrainian dialect, a dialect that Ukrainians in Ukraine criticize. But a more important reason for not taking them to learn Ukrainian is that my boys choose to do sports on Saturdays and not Ukrainian language classes. At work, my brain is in the English gear. I work as a part-time adjunct instructor, but as all adjuncts know, there is no such thing as teaching part-time. All my class prep is done at home. While at home, I have to put dinner on the table, do laundry, and take care of the cleaning, so my Ukrainian language "hour" with my children is reduced to about 20 minutes.

It is a constant struggle. My brain is doing all the thinking and talking in English, so switching to Ukrainian is hard. I'm forgetting words and choosing silence instead of communicating with my kids. Then it hits me. The reason language exists is for relationships, to communicate love, and to develop your children's understanding of the world, not to insist on one language. I can't achieve these things by insisting on speaking in Ukrainian.

Here's one concrete example. Julian is four and I'm driving to his preschool at Bethel University (where I work) and we stop at a red light. I am trying to explain to him about the snowplows and other trucks at the intersection. I don't remember how to say snowplows because we didn't have them in Buzhanka. Saying "truck" isn't specific enough. A truck that removes the snow is too long. My brain just can't find all the words. So, I sit there in silence, frustrated at myself. And I immediately realize that the depth of the conversation is compromised by trying to persist in one particular language. I want my communication with my children to be effortless and playful, but it is a challenge. That struggle is compounded by the fact that I am the only one speaking that language and that I can't find the words when I need them. There was no word for a screwdriver in Ukrainian and I grew up saying отвьортка or *otvyortka*, a *Surzhik* word, which is based on a loan word from Russian. There was no Ukrainian word for an extension cord, so we said тройнік or *troynik*, the three-plug thing-y. The list goes on.

When Ukrainian purists make the effort to purify the language from Russian influences, Ukrainians were happy to use English loan words to replace the words borrowed from Russian. Anything but Russian was their decision. One example was the word for helicopter. I grew up saying вертоліт, *vertolit,* or вертольот, *vertolyot* in *Surzhik,* but the new word is гелікоптер, *helikopter,* which is basically the English word helicopter written in Cyrillic. The word for train I knew was поїзд, *poyizd*, which was replaced by a brand-new word no one in Central Ukraine ever heard: потяг, *potyah.*

It would be interesting to research this to see the origins of the new words. I bet some of them are from Western Ukraine, a region with a more nationalistic spirit that is filled with Ukrainians who were braver and spoke Ukrainian with pride. People in Western Ukraine tend to be more nationalistic because their lands had once been taken over by Poland and Austria, so they are more fervent about their Ukrainian identity and this is manifested through language.

But here's what language purists who are working hard on cleaning up the Ukrainian language from Russian influences are ignoring the reality that Ukrainians who live in the borderlands with Romania and Hungary and Poland have their own *Surzhik* which mixes Ukrainian with Romanian, Hungarian, and Polish in their respective regions. Languages intermix because people intermix and no committee can stop the evolution of language.

Robbed Of One's Own History

I am an adjunct at Bethel University, and Julian is two years old. I have an opportunity to develop a course called Ukrainian Language and Culture. My course syllabus involves trips to St. Katherine's Ukrainian Orthodox Church, the Church of Evangelical Christian Baptists in St. Louis Park, and the Ukrainian gift store, among other experiences.

The textbook I choose for the class is *Borderland*, by Anne Reid. As I sit in my office leafing through the book to develop the syllabus, I am struck by the most profound sense of loss. I realize I don't know the history of my own land. I sit there and cry. I don't know how to process my feelings. I haven't used the lens of "colonizer" and "colonized" in relation to Ukraine and the Soviet Union. I thought it pertained only to India or African countries, but not to Ukraine. Ukraine wasn't really colonized by anyone. But in a way, it was. Our language, our land, our identity were colonized by Soviet ideology, Russian language, and Soviet identity.

I left Ukraine in 1995 and my coursework in college in Ukraine included one textbook by Orest Subtelniy on the history of Ukraine, but we devoted more time to the history of the Communist Party than to my own country that has existed for thousands of years (no exaggeration there). I grew up learning that Russia was great and Russia was *великая Россия (velikaya Rossiya) or* Great Russia, and that Ukraine was but a borderland, a land in-between, a land that lay in the way of others passing through. Can you imagine the impact on people having grown up in a land that was nothing but a hindrance or something to take advantage of? From Americans, I heard it was referred to as "the Breadbasket of Europe," something I never heard growing up. Maybe, "Breadbasket of the Soviet Union" since our rich fields could feed tens of millions for two years with one year's crops. But I wonder if they meant "Breadbasket FOR Europe" since we hold the richest *chernozem* (black earth) and we exported tons of wheat to Europe. Our wheat fields birthed the inspiration for the Ukrainian flag, with blue for the sky and yellow for the wheat fields.

While I reside in the U.S., I relive being from "part of Russia" every time someone asks me, "Where are you from?" and I say, "Ukraine." They proceed to ask me, "Do you know Natasha from St. Petersburg? She lives in Saint Louis Park. There is a huge Russian community there." I proceed to tell them patiently, "I've never been to Russia. I'm from Ukraine." Then they tell me about their trips in the '80s to Moscow. People start talking about Russia every time I answer their question about where I'm from. It happens almost every time in the first ten years of my immigration to the U.S.. Finally when Ukraine shows up in the international news, especially with the Maidan Revolution of 2014, I am being recognized as a Ukrainian from Ukraine.

I do have a plea to all of you who used to associate Ukraine with Russia (it's not only Americans). Don't erase us from the map twice. The first time was during the Cold War when your government, history books, and news agencies didn't make a distinction or recognize us as a people with a history, an identity, and a language. And today, when someone says they're from Ukraine, take a moment and consider that Ukraine has been invaded by Russia three times, that Russia has killed tens of millions of our people, and that we are currently fighting against Russian forces that have invaded our country, trying to take it over again before you say, "I know someone from Russia" or "I've been to Russia. But I know it's not the same thing."

Just don't say those words. Much better is to say, "Nice to meet you. You are the first Ukrainian I've ever met," or something like that. The equivalent is when you say, "I'm from Michigan," I could say, "I know someone from Kentucky. I've been to Kentucky before. I know it's not the same as Michigan, but great people."

Google Translate To the Rescue

Given the elaborate explanations about why my children are not bilingual, I hope there is more understanding than judgment why my children speak and understand so little of their mother's tongue. But they are very creative and inventive communicators! My husband and I are in Ukraine with our children and they use Google Translate. Nicky uses it with his Grandma Nadia to ask when dinner will be ready when I'm not around to translate. He also takes his phone to the local shop to get some treats. Not being able to speak Ukrainian isn't a barrier for him. He relies on technology to meet his needs.

When visiting my brother, their uncle, in Amsterdam, Nicky learns all kinds of GPS directions in Ukrainian when Bogdan switches the navigation system to Ukrainian. *Поверніть ліворуч (povernit livoruch)*, "turn left," and *Поверніть праворуч (povernit pravoruch)*, "turn right." His favorite one was *povernit livoruch*, "turn left," so he teaches his friends how to say it. I can hear them play Overwatch and say *Поверніть ліворуч*, po-ver-nit lee-vo-rooch. It must have become a code language for something like, "My mom's here, watch out."

It does break my heart I wasn't strong enough to insist on Ukrainian. Hindsight is 20/20. I comfort myself with knowing that my children are interested in Ukraine. They love Ukraine. They choose to research Ukraine as their topic for research papers in middle school. They choose to report on the annexation of Crimea by the Russians and bring in live experiences of actually being there before it was occupied.

My heart also grows warm when I see my children try to communicate with my parents. If the desire to communicate and develop a relationship is there, people find all kinds of ways to figure out how to exchange messages and get their ideas out to each other. I'm proud to say that my children have that desire. I've seen children who speak the same language as their grand-parents and yet do not reach out to communicate with them. The barrier to relationships is not always the language.

Remembering Ukraine: Nicky's Account

We are are at the airport in Ukraine. Grandpa Tolya is overjoyed to see his daughter, our mom, and pleased to see us. He gives me a kiss on the cheek which surprised me, but I get over it soon, remembering a video from my Spanish class where kisses are an accepted cultural thing for greetings in countries like France and Spain. We are driving in a little car, sitting on small beige benches in the rear of the car, almost cuddling with the luggage.

After a four-hour drive, we see a house. It's old and vintage looking. I meet my grandma, Baba Nadia. Her face lights up and she gives me a big warm hug. I say "Privet," because that's the only greet-ing I know. She gives me a kiss on the cheek and says something in Ukrainian that I smile and nod my head to. I see two cats: one is named Ryzhiy (red cat) and the other one Ryzhik (little red cat). I try to pick up Ryzhik and he bites me. They show me the room where I'll be sleeping and it has a clock that runs eight hours ahead of what I'm used to.

There is a large green wooden wall separating the family area and the farm area behind the house. We go through a small door to the farm and I see the animals. I walk in and on my left, I see an area closed off by a metal chain fence, like ones securing a high school

football field. There are eggs on the ground and it surprises me. Of course, I know that chickens lay eggs, but I was never shown the real process of how chickens lay eggs, instead of just a carton with a dozen eggs inside. I see the chickens and then we meet the rooster. My mom translates Grandpa Tolya's warning me that the rooster is angry and can take out my eye. We go into the back area of the farm where the animals sleep, eat, and poop. I learned I have to watch where I step. I immediately see the baby goat cowering in the corner of

Nicky with Ryzhyk, Summer 2017.

its pen, and ask my Grandpa Tolya to pet it. My brother and I slowly stroll over to the mother and a baby goat. While the baby goat is scared of us, the mother protects her child by ramming forward when we attempt to pet the goats, but the mom's leash takes her back.

A couple of days after, Dad and I head out to a market, about a 15-minute walk away. We walk into this small, dark 7-11 type store and I look for a snack to buy. I pull out the translate app on my phone and type in, "What do you recommend?" and translate it to Ukrainian. The shopkeeper at the register looks confused but takes the phone and types a response back using a Ukrainian keyboard. It says, "What kind, desserts, snacks?" I tell her snacks and she turns around, picks up two bags of chips, and hands them to me. The bags have Cyrillic writing on them so I ask my dad what it means. He doesn't know. I know that there's something on my translator that can take pictures of foreign text and replace it with English, so I try it. It takes a couple of tries but the app eventually shows that the chips she gave me are mushroom and sour cream chips. A bit unusual in the U.S., but I'm not in the U.S., so I buy them.

We return from our market trip with our snacks and my grandpa asks me if I would like to help him feed the chickens. I am hesitant at first, but my parents insist that I do it. We head to the back area and pass the goats, heading into a small feeding pen where there's a trough, ready to get filled with a mixture of corn and other grains. Grandpa gives me a handful of chicken food and tells me to hand it out to them and put it in the trough. My hand goes out and my fear goes up when the chickens start rushing toward the food. I get pecked on my finger and accidentally drop all of the food. I rush toward my mom and tell her that my finger hurts, and I feel really bad for dropping the food. I pull a Band-Aid out of my backpack and a small tube of Neosporin and put both on my finger.

Ukraine is my mother's home country and will forever welcome me. I'm thankful for the trip that my family took and that I could learn about the culture of Ukraine, and where my roots come from.

Remembering Ukraine: Julian's Account

In total, I have been to Ukraine four separate times, two of which were when I was 1 ½ and 2 ½ years old. I don't remember much those first times. Things I actually remember are from when I went when I was 6, still not a lot, but some good memories. One memory is of me hanging out with Did Tolya. Another one is of me participating in the vareniky eating contest in Zolo. I won the contest and they gave me a wooden spoon as my prize! The other memory is from me biking down the hill in front of my grandparents' house on a decently nice day. I don't remember exactly what happened, but somehow I fell

*off my bike and ended up scraping both my knees. I was quite sure
that was it for my life, but instead, I must have gotten up, sobbing of
course, and got patched up by my mom. The other thing I remember
was when my cousin Dima made me a wooden plane, with nails as its*

*wheels, painted silver for me to
play with. We still have it today
and it's a great memory of that
trip.*

*Our most recent trip, in 2017,
was quite memorable. We walk
down to the market store and
buy some cheap bottles of coke,
"corn-puffs" (called corn
sticks), sunflower seeds, chips,
etc. It is fun to walk down there,
talk with Mom and Dad about
the memories they had of the
area. We meet with my mom's
cousin Kolya's family, talk with
them, and take a shortcut back*

My dad and Julian by the cherry tree by
our house, July 2003.

*to the house. Later we spend a couple of hours before bed, eating
sunflower seeds, talking with grandma and grandpa about almost
anything. Those nights are the most memorable.*

*Another day we go down to the quarry with our cousins, Ihor and
Dima. While we are swimming in the quarry, they put some pork on
the grill, and we come back up to dry off and eat some chips along
with the "shashlik.". Later, Nicky and I help Grandpa whom I cal
Did Tolya gather straw and leaves to feed the pigs. We first go down
by some of the neighbors' houses, and later we gather some closer to
the house. Then I help him with fixing the garden hydration system,
which for me, meant holding a metal piece for like 20 minutes.*

One Sunday we drive to Did Tolya's church, where he is a pastor, and help set it up and waited for the members to come in. I get to meet a lot of the regular attendees and listen to Did Tolya speak, with my mom translating into English (just for me and Nicky), and then my dad gives a sermon. Even though we are only there for a week, I get so much more out of it than the last three trips and get to know my grandparents a lot better.

My kids may not have learned to speak Ukrainian but they have learned to love the Ukrainian people, the culture, and the mushroom sour cream potato chips.

My dad preaching at his church.

CHAPTER 16

"How Do You Say Your Name Again?"

It's not even 8 a.m. on a Tuesday morning, and I'm already at the Atlanta International Airport on my way home from a keynote speaker gig at a teacher's conference. My brain tires from the conference that lasts over the weekend. I quickly fly through security with my TSA PreCheck card because money can buy that for you in America. You can obtain a "known traveler" status for $100 and I'm reminded that in Ukraine, there is no such thing. I bet in Ukraine "TSA PreCheck" is only available to the oligarchs or, as Dad reminded me, they don't need a pre-check because they fly their own planes to grab lunch in Paris using the extorted money that our elderly pensioners are still waiting for, as promised in the elections.

Corruption and inequality stir up my inner sense of justice every time I come across one or the other. My mind constantly juxtaposes and analyzes my beloved homeland of Ukraine, the way I know her, the way I love her, and the way I hate her corruption all at the same time. To be an immigrant is to always live in the between, or be constantly present in both. To be an immigrant is to be constantly conscious, as Eva Hoffman says in her memoir "*Lost in Translation*." With these thoughts, I find my way to the gate. Once there, I am reminded of my under-caffeination, so I make my way to get a coffee.

Some days I just want to be invisible, to blend in, to be like everyone else (whatever that means), and not to draw attention to myself, to my "cute" accent, or my name. This is one of those "wanting to be invisible" days at the airport in Atlanta. I order coffee and a croissant at an airport coffee shop, hoping to quickly pick up my order and disappear. I even put Bose noise-canceling headphones on, working hard to tune people out. It turns out that my name is going to slow down this whole escape, darn it. I wait for the coffee and three feet away I hear this, "Her name is weird." The barista turns and looks at me and says, "If your order is called and you can't recognize it, there is a number on your receipt." I tell her, "I'm not a number. I have a name." "Your name is weird," she explains her reasoning.

I'm so glad she's taking the time to explain why I need to refer to the number on my receipt in the event my name is butchered. I say to her, "It's not weird. It's Roos-LAH-nah." "Well, I didn't mean it that way," she responds, immediately regretting her mistake. I wonder for a second, with my blood pressure rising and not being hungry anymore, *How exactly did you mean it?* But I don't want to be the provocateur because then the whole Ukrainian ethnicity will be painted as rude and provocative if we actually try to challenge these name-butchering practices. I choose the polite route. I silently grab my food and I turn to leave. *"So much for being invisible,"* I think to myself.

A guy who has been watching everything offers, "Your name is beautiful." I recognize that in my new home called America, my name is weird *and* beautiful at the same time, on the same day. I love this America again and try to find the silver lining in this situation because being negative and having an attitude is frowned upon. "Stay positive," says the voice of positive, polite white people in my head, but my own voice says, "Call it like it is. Don't sugarcoat it. When you do that, you minimize the microaggressions." You find fault with yourself and your name and your accent and how you can't beat around the bush and how you don't hide your emotions because you were raised to be open, authentic, and a straight shooter.

In the meantime, I'm working on an alias for all my coffee orders. I might go with Natasha. Or maybe if I feel like Mary, Sara, or Jessica, I'll be one of those. I definitely need better options for those days when I want to blend in.

It's February 21, 1973, five days after I am born. In Ukraine, mothers stay in the hospital longer than in America. (My mom was shocked to hear I was kicked out two days after my C-section when I had Julian in an American hospital). My mom brings me home from the hospital swaddled so tight, I can't move my arms. The road home is long because there was a snowstorm on February 16th. My dad isn't present for the birth because this is not a common practice. He only comes to pick her up and waits outside.

I come home from the hospital without a name. There is no pressure to name a baby in the hospital. My sister looks at me and sees me for the first time. She names me Ruslana. I'm not sure of the origin. She once told me that she heard it on the radio or it was the name of a famous singer in the '70s or a poet. But she is not alive now for me to ask her for more details. I wish I had, though, before she passed away on my birthday in 2001. It's a rare name in Ukraine and very easy to pronounce. I'm told it means "lioness," and my husband would agree.

Now the name is becoming more popular in Ukraine because of the famous singer Ruslana Lyzhychko who won the Eurovision contest in 2004 and is known mononymously as Ruslana. It becomes very obvious to me that it is not easy to pronounce when I arrive in the United States. Some people are audacious enough to say, "Nice to meet you, Ruth." I cringe because I didn't invite them to call me Ruth. There is no "th" sound in Ukrainian. To say that sound would be considered *некультурно (nekulturno) or* uncultured, according to the rules I was raised with. When you say *th*, you have to stick your tongue out. It's almost like what you do when you are getting ready to spit. But I know that sticking your tongue out and spitting are things only uncultured people do. My mom tells me this when I am 5 or 6. Then I come to America, and here, people have a sound that makes you stick your tongue out and then quickly hide it. I visualize a snake flicking its tongue, sensing its surroundings.

Every time I introduce myself in the United States, it is never a quick, "Hi, Ruslana. Nice to meet you." The introduction goes on for a while because people are nice and work hard to learn my name. They want me to say it again. Then the whole conversation is about my name and where I'm from and not about the issue we were going to discuss. I repeat it again and I learn quickly that people often miss the *R* at the beginning because it's not rolled in English, so my name sounds like Uslana. I proceed to spell my name and soon learn that it doesn't help. I try writing out my name, thinking that visual reinforcement can speed up the process. It often works, if I can find a piece of paper and a pen in my purse, where all things are swallowed up like a black hole.

Then I try another strategy. "My name is Ruslana, starts with an *R*," I say, as if it is my Indian name, Stands with a Fist. Some people just feel embarrassed that they didn't catch it, so they don't say back, "Hi, Ruslana." They just say, "Hi." I understand their pain because I have problems pronouncing Vietnamese or Chinese names because my articulatory system was not formed using those sounds and I have difficulty distinguishing tonal sounds.

I waste some time scrolling through Facebook and see this meme that says, "If you can pronounce names like Tchaikovsky, Dostoyevsky, and Michelangelo, then you can pronounce other names." I know that people aren't intentionally trying to mispronounce names. It really does come down to someone's articulatory system and the phonological environment that shaped it. Longer names are not necessarily harder. Dostoyevsky, Tchaikovsky, and Michelangelo are names from Indo-European languages. To an Indo-European monolingual ear, Korean and Vietnamese names are truly phonologically different. From a sociolinguistic point of view, it is important to acknowledge that, in some cases, the causes of mispronunciation stem from racist attitudes. Those mispronunciations are worth questioning. But for those Americans who are trying to understand what my name is and pronounce it correctly, but are struggling to do so, I say, "Thank you for trying."

In church, during "greet your neighbor" time, the pastor assigns us a topic to discuss as an icebreaker, as if we are all in second grade. My husband chafes at the thought of having to exchange topics with people every Sunday and is considering volunteering in the sound booth just to avoid it. The topics include such deep theological issues as your favorite donut, whether you drink your coffee black or with cream, your favorite winter/spring/summer/fall activity, and whether or not you're a fan of Daylight Saving Time. We don't dare talk about whether you are a Packers or a Vikings fan because that will lead to division in the church, and we are working so hard on maintaining "unity in the midst of diversity."

But I think they are missing the point that having a sprinkling of Steelers and Vikings fans in the body actually contributes to the diversity of Packers-loving Wisconsin. No topics that are borderline political are discussed either, so donuts, weather, and sports are the safety zones. Right before we turn and talk to our neighbor, I want to go refill my coffee and say hi to people who know how to pronounce my name and with whom I can have a conversation beyond donuts and weather and sports, but I'm supposed to make new friends and build community. So, I engage in this small talk, hoping that it will lead to deeper relationships, but it doesn't. Anyone who has a deep relationship with another person doesn't waste time on small talk.

We rarely get to the assigned topic because people are working so hard on pronouncing my name, which leads to, "Where are you from?" Often the greeting is extended with, "I love your accent. Where is your accent from?" I want to say "I'm from Ukraine but my accent is from Minnesota." I resist. Instead, I do the polite thing. By the time we are done answering those questions, it's time to sit down and watch the announcements on the screen. I don't really regret not having a chance to share about my favorite donut. I have a lot more success at discussing the favorite donut topic on those days when I volunteer at the info desk because I get to wear a nametag and people can see my name. The visual reinforcement clarifies the presence of an *R* at the beginning of my name, and on those days I am not called Uslana, Luslana or Rushlana.

My dad, my brother, and my husband call me Ru. In addition, there are other people in my inner circle who are invited to call me Ru. They are my friends and co-workers. The circle is ever expanding but it never shrinks, unless people like my sister and my mom stop saying it because they are gone from this earth.

I hear my mom use the endearing name *Ruslanochka* where the suffix *-ochka* adds a loving meaning to my name. For a boy, the suffix is *-chik* as in *Bohdanchik*, a term of endearment for my brother. In America, the endearing suffix is replaced with honey and sweetheart, and I love both of these words, using both, *Robchik* and Honey Rob.

People often ask me what my middle name is. I don't have a short answer to that question. It's not even a middle name, technically. It is only called my middle name because it's between my first name and my last name, but not in the way it's defined in the U.S. There is no such thing as Ruslana Maria Westerlund. My middle name is my father's name with a suffix indicating I am his daughter. His name is Anatoliy. It is a common Ukrainian name, derived from the Greek name *Ανατολιος, Anatolios*, meaning sunrise. So, I carry a bit of sunrise in me. I carry a bit of my dad in me. Anatoliy+ivna=Anatoliyivna.

But transliteration is never as straightforward as writing down sound-letter correspondence. Sometimes, my dad's name is transliterated as Anatoli. The Russian pronunciation of my middle name and the way it was written in the passport earns me a reward for having the longest middle name with 12 letters total. But I carry it proudly because every time I spell it, I am reminded that I am my father's daughter.

CHAPTER 17

"What Do You Remember Most About Your Mom?"

Sorting Through Memories and Regrets

"I wish you knew how much of you there is in everything I do. It can be the smallest thing ... trivial ... mundane ... but you're there, under the surface of it somewhere. I wish you knew how I can I carry you with me always ... Everywhere I go." — Ranata Suzuki

W hat do I remember the most about you? Your passion for everything you did, from doing the dishes to visiting the sick to caring for the orphans and the poor widows in Vynograd and Buzhanka. You were Christ to them. You also loved Jesus with every fiber of your being. You weren't afraid of the Gospel because the Gospel was the source of your salvation. As you served the people alongside Dad, you preached the Gospel and, occasionally, you used words. You also had zeal in mundane things. And now I carry your passion forward. I carry

My mom and I at our house in Minnesota.

you forward in my daily activities. Mom, you are there when I do the dishes. You are there when I dry my hands on a towel and when I hang the towel to dry. I thought you were mainly with me in the kitchen. And yes, it's true that you are with me when I sauté onions, when I stir the soup, when I taste my borsch, when I julienne the carrots, when I put the lid back on and watch it closely so it won't spill over. But you are most felt in the garden when I tend to my vegetables and flowers.

It's Saturday morning and I am working in my garden and I rally everybody to help me pull weeds. They all work for about four hours nonstop, but still, we aren't done. I keep going until the work is finished. Rob tells me, "Your mom lives on in you when you work hard. Your mom lives on when you don't quit." I have always been like that because you taught me to work first and rest later.

I remember you in little things and in big things. The memories are not in any order but they all surge like a wave or drip like rain drops on a rainy summer day. Do I start with the time of being a rebellious teen or the reconciliatory talk we had in Crimea? Or do I write about how much you loved roses and how lovely they were in your garden or the dozens of rose bouquets people laid on your coffin burning red in front of my eyes? Why do the funeral memories interfere and take over my memories of you, the living mom? How do I write about your life when your death overwhelms my memory? How do I move forward without being able to talk to you and, in return, see your eyes full of love and joy? The only way I can communicate with you now is through these pages and this ink, there are no words to exchange with you and hear your voice again. I feel sad, but my friends tell me to share happy memories, so I will do both. I will tell happy memories, overcome with grief that doesn't go away.

Mom, do you know that I have the same roses as yours in my garden? I feel like you speak through them to me. I return to the U.S. from your funeral with overwhelming grief that feels like a heavy rock in my stomach and on my chest and I go to my garden. I gaze at the flowers in search of peace and my eyes come to rest on the roses. I realize they are exactly the same ones as in your garden. A sense of calm and peace comes over me. I feel as if you say, "I'm here with you." Yours are better cared for. Yours grow well-supported on the trellis, mine spill out on the ground. I don't know why I didn't notice them there before. Maybe it's because I didn't travel in June, the month when roses are in full bloom, or maybe we were too busy cooking and eating when we were there. Or maybe it's because I didn't visit often enough.

After your passing, I regret having emigrated in the first place. I think to myself that if I hadn't, if I had stayed close to you, I would have kept cancer at bay. I think that maybe, by staying in Ukraine, I could have somehow kept you from dying. I also regret getting my doctorate because I spent all my vacation days on my classes or writing my dissertation instead of visiting you and seeing you alive. Now I have a doctorate but I lost you. What have I gained? I have gained a great loss.

In my deep grief, I regret much about America. In this deep grief, it is hard for me to justify reasons for my emigration, when I lost you, when I wasn't there to hold your hand and say goodbye, when you died alone in the hospital. But then I remember. I remember that you wanted me to go to America. You wanted a better life for me. So, see, mom, after all, I am your obedient daughter.

These memories are most precious.

You are in Minnesota and Nicky is just a baby. Julian is 4. The boys have this fire truck with a ladder attached to it. You play with Nicky with that truck and Nicky keeps pushing the button and the sound comes out saying, "Extend the ladder." It makes me laugh when I come home from work and you say to me, "Listen to what I learned today: Extenda ladda. Extenda ladda." That's how you learned English. You started speaking English in complete sentences from day one. You also learned to say "Good job" and "Thank you" and "I love you" because those phrases were used frequently in our home.

Mom with Julian and Nicky, Spring 2006.

Now we are in your flower garden in Buzhanka. You are picking raspberries for Julian and he eats them out of your hand. Julian is about 3 years old. You take him with you to the chickens to gather eggs and Julian carries them carefully in the fold of his sweater and happily tells me, "Mom, look how many eggs the chickens gave us!" Then you are making an omelet for Julian and he loves the way you make it with milk. It always rises and it's very fluffy and you talk to him in Ukrainian and he understands you and feels the love in your voice and in the twinkle of your eyes.

Mom, I remember you in so many ways—your direct bold way of talking, your fervent prayers for my children, your stubbornness, and your controlling tendencies in the kitchen that I inherited. I inherited all of it. That's *moya spadshchina,* my inheritance from you. So many people who look at me tell me I look just like you. I love the sound of that. We had our tense moments in our relationship and I hated myself for being such a rebellious daughter. But we also had our moments of reconciliation, which I hope every mother and daughter who have had a tense relationship will have.

Reconciling with Our Past and Ourselves

Mom, remember those times when I rebelled against you and the only way you knew how to handle that was the way your dad did? The cycle of yelling and hitting that you grew up with never left. It was the only way you knew how to teach me to be obedient. Obedience was so important to you, but I couldn't be obedient by force. I was young and free-willed and I rebelled and lied to you, but every time I did, you found out. What followed next was you teaching me obedience. I learned about the importance of telling the truth from you through your physical punishment. Mom, you knew that it didn't work but you didn't know any other way. We are victims of the way we were raised but we don't have to stay there. But I didn't know that you didn't know any other way, until the time we had our talk on our first Ukrainian family vacation in 2004.

We are in Crimea and we stay with Tyotya Halya. Natasha, my sister-in-law, is there. Julian is 3.5 years old and Diana, Bogdan and Natasha's daughter, is 1.5 years old. I don't remember what leads to the conversation. We are in the kitchen. Kitchens are the place for deep talk. Everything is discussed in the kitchen from government corruption to local gossip. I think we are discussing marriage. In the hours that pass, we end up talking about the verbal and physical abuse in your childhood and how you didn't know any other way to raise me to be obedient. Our reconciliation process starts with "Forgive me" uttered on both sides, one side of control and another side of rebellion. It is the only family vacation we ever took and it created a new relationship between me and you.

Mom, you know that I love you and I forgave you. And I thank you for forgiving me. I see you in the Boryspil airport waving goodbye and asking for forgiveness again, saying *"Probach meni*, Ruslanochka, *Probach meni dotsiu.* Forgive me, Ruslana, forgive me, my daughter." In that act of seeking and giving forgiveness, you teach me humbleness, how to forgive and how to love, and how to live forgiven. I learn through this process that reconciliation happens not when "Forgive me" is uttered but when we decide that abusive cycles must stop, and negative behaviors from our families of origin have no place in our new families. We are able to reconcile because Jesus forgave us first. He offers us forgiveness every day. We must reach out to Him and find peace with God and ourselves. It is with Jesus that I live forgiven and can forgive others.

I'm writing about this openly and vulnerably because I believe if we talk about our past, we can learn from our humanness. If we can learn lessons from our prior history, we can prevent repeating it. By admitting our mistakes, we can face them more boldly. We can openly admit that we are only human and being human means being inherently flawed. We all have issues, it's just that some of us are already aware and others aren't yet aware.

In my case and in the case of my mom, we tackled our past, we examined the root causes, and we reclaimed a relationship based on love and not based on control. The only regret I have is not talking to my mom often enough, not calling her more frequently, because reconciliation is a lifelong pursuit. But I will have an eternity with mom where we won't be obsessing about our past, but living in harmony, reconciled with ourselves and our Creator. That reconciliation will be complete, whole, and perfect.

Ukrainian Funerals

Ukrainian funerals, similar to all funerals, are emotionally challenging to live through and even harder to talk about. Unlike American funerals I have experienced, in Ukraine, there are no funeral homes. The body comes home in a coffin and stays there for visitation and funeral. The coffin is placed in the least occupied and coolest room inside the house in the winter, or on the porch in the summer to keep the body cool. Two of the hardest funerals I ever experienced were when I buried my sister and when I buried my mother. When the body comes home, the grief is so unbearable that my stomach hurts and my brain doesn't register or remember hunger. The closeness of the body makes it hard to breathe, think, and exist. In the U.S., the body is left in the funeral home and you return to your empty house to grieve, which is undoubtedly very hard. In Ukraine, the body is in the home. It's in your living room, right there with you.

When my sister died from lung cancer at the age of 31, her husband Volodya came to Buzhanka for the funeral. No, we didn't put him up in a hotel. The expectation is that relatives stay with relatives, not as strangers in a hotel.

He stayed with us. The coffin was in the living room where Volodya slept, in the same room, but he spent the night on the couch. The grief is so heavy, you can almost see it like a thick, suffocating smog. Can you imagine the experience? Can you feel the feelings in that room? Can you smell the formaldehyde coming off the dead body? The most difficult thing when dealing with the death of a loved one is having their mortal remains lying in your living room.

Think of the contrast between how different cultures handle the dead body and the emotions around it. Look at the meaning of space and distance and what they communicate. In America, most relatives don't have to manage the body. They distance themselves from it and the emotions that swallow them up. In Ukraine, the body is in your living room. You are close to it, you deal with the emotions as they come when you walk by the body and see those sealed lips and the arms crossed over the chest and the eyes that are closed, not letting you look into them one more time.

I guess I have become too American because I prefer funeral homes. I still want to spend more time with Mom's body, looking at her face and holding her hands. But you really can't hold her hands because they are cold and they don't squeeze back. You touch them and it feels like you are touching cold cement. And I still want her to spend her last night in her beautiful home where she lived for 50 years. At that point, she was already with Jesus where there are no tears, crying, cancer, or diabetes. The reason I prefer funeral homes is because the process is exhausting for the family. My brother and dad bring the coffin home and I see that they are too busy to grieve. Mom died at 10 p.m. on Wednesday. My dad asked the morgue to hold her until Friday to accommodate my transatlantic trip for the funeral on Saturday. They pick up her body and drive home immediately to my village, three hours away, in the scorching heat. The physical and emotional toll drains all of their energy.

They are working hard to make sure the body is transported respectfully. When they get home, they don't sit down to talk. They barely stop for a hug. They have to take the coffin off the truck and carry it down the steep driveway that mom loved sweeping and keeping clean because Ruslana has arrived (*Руслана приїхала*). They are running around making sure the body is rested in a ventilated place because it is one of the hottest Junes in Ukraine, and the stupid Ukrainian morgue attendants forget to embalm the body. So, Dad arranges to keep the body cool by asking his neighbors to use empty Pepsi bottles to freeze water to put below the coffin until the funeral the next day. Can you imagine worrying about how to keep your mother's body from decomposing while you wallow in grief? You pay the price of not having funeral homes and correcting people's mistakes who forget to embalm the body. Ukrainian people live in a system that's killing them, literally.

I get the call that Mom passed away while I'm on vacation. I'm in the middle of a family celebratory dinner that we all have been looking forward to since last summer. We are celebrating my father-in-law's 80th birthday and are on the Outer Banks, North Carolina. I scramble to get my passport Fedexed to New York, catch a flight to JFK, and manage to arrive in Ukraine the day before her funeral. The body isn't home yet. My cousin picks me up and brings me home from the airport. I arrive in Buzhanka at 8 p.m. I get out of the car outside the gates to our house and will never forget the moment of going down the driveway toward the house knowing my mom isn't there to greet me.

She isn't there to hold my face in her hands and kiss me on both cheeks three times and tell me how much she missed me and how hard she prayed that God would make this moment possible. There are no kisses, no tears of joy, no words of thanksgiving. All I see is the absence of mom. The emptiness in the *podvirya* (driveway) is so heavy. Mom always came out to the *podvirya* to greet me. Always.

I stand there in that empty place where we would kiss and feel the deepest emptiness engulf me. The meaning of heaviness follows me for about a month every night at 8 p.m., especially after returning back to the States.

I finally figure out why. It was the time when I felt it in my deepest core that the umbilical cord that connected me with my mom was cut again. But not forever, because those who die in Jesus will be reunited with Jesus and each other again. Our bodies may fail, but our spirits live on. We pass over. I don't say it as a platitude. I say it because I believe in the resurrected Jesus and our future resurrected bodies.

When the coffin arrives, I run to hug my dad and my brother. There is nothing I can say, so I let the grip of the embrace say it all. My dad's eyes are sunken deep into the hollows and he looks like he aged ten years in one day. He's lost weight. His shirt hangs on him like on a hanger. My brother's eyes are red and puffy from crying. My dad and my brother lived through this once before. They brought my sister home in a coffin all the way from Rivne, a city 500 miles away. It's too much to bear. How does a husband live through this? How can a son bring home his mother's body in a coffin?

The visitation in Ukraine is another lesson in cultural contrasts. Visitations aren't scheduled at a particular time at the funeral home before the memorial service. There are no invitations. Neighbors come and visit with the body, standing quietly and solemnly with their heads bowed and hands folded. The subtle nodding of the head silently says hello to the bereaved, but no words are exchanged. There are no conversations with the survivors, no matter how long it's been since you've seen them or even if you have something to say. In fact, it's not even called a visitation. You just know that the coffin is home and that it's the respectful thing to do.

The day of the funeral begins with people coming from all over the neighborhood. They bring flowers upon flowers, and my job is to find room for them. Mom loved roses. I place some roses on her coffin but they roll off. I put some in the 3- and 2-liter jars, the same jars she used for canning my favorite apples in a sugary syrup. I take those jars and fill them with water and put flowers in so they will stay fresh for Mom as if she were there to enjoy them. Many of the things we do during the funeral are for the living, not for the dead. It's our way of honoring them. But I catch myself wondering if Mom would like flowers by her feet or by her head. The decisions are numerous and you find yourself not being able to make the simplest of them. People keep coming and more flowers are coming.

Then the wailing begins. Wailing is just something you do. I already cried out all my tears Wednesday through Friday. Today is Saturday and I have no tears left. Tyotya Tosia, mom's sister, starts wailing, my brother cries so hard and talks to Mom, sobbing. I've never seen or heard him cry like that. When our sister died, there was more wailing because she was so young and had left two boys behind, ages 9 and 11. The boys only recently told me how the wailing and the loud music from the funeral band scared them and it wasn't helpful for them. But wailing is something you do, otherwise, people will think you aren't sad enough for their passing.

There are dozens of Orthodox rituals one of my aunts is reminding us to follow, but we don't because my dad and I don't believe that the rituals are going to help the dead. They are for the living Orthodox. As Evangelical Christians, we believe that the spirit is already with Jesus. To comfort myself, I say out loud that Mom is already with Jesus and my aunt corrects me and instructs me that the spirit roams the earth for 40 days. I tell her the Bible doesn't say that and quickly realize we must not be reading the same Bible. I don't want to argue, but I refuse to follow Orthodox rituals. I go inside the house and the covered mirrors remind me we have a *pokoinik*, the deceased. Covering the mirrors is another tradition we reluctantly follow. My dad doesn't believe in spirits and covering mirrors, but his sister, my Tyotya Tosia, makes sure the Orthodox rituals are obeyed.

After about an hour, the procession starts when the truck arrives. The truck for transporting the coffin is not a closed hearse, but an open-air flatbed truck. I am reminded that even this practice of the coffin on the truck bed tells us how people in different cultures are expected to handle death. Ukrainians handle all the elements of death in the open. Americans hide the death by giving the body over to the funeral home staff, and allowing other people to handle the body, dig the grave, and transport the deceased.

The truck bed is lined with velvet cloth and a large ornate rug, including plastic funeral flowers. Strong men step out from the crowd to take the coffin and carefully lift it up on the truck. Two kids are positioned to walk in front of the truck. They are my niece and nephew, my brother's kids. They were assigned this job at the last minute and I can see how confused they are to do this task. Their job is to drop cut-up papers on the ground, marking the way for the dead body to the cemetery. I bet it's some type of superstition for the spirit to find its way to the afterlife. Dad and I do not believe in these things but the pressure from the aunts and the village is strong. If disobeyed, there will be judgment from the village later.

"They didn't bury Nadya correctly," they will later gossip. "She will not end up in heaven," the people will judge. But we know that it was my mom's relationship with the resurrected Jesus that reconciled her with the living God, and our salvation is not earned by following these rituals, but it is the gift of God. It can't be earned, so no one can boast that they followed the rituals by covering up the mirrors and sprinkling paper confetti on the ground.

The band plays extremely mournful funeral music which makes people cry and wail again. People line up following the truck. The closest family goes first. My brother sobs, "Mom, you loved walking on this road to go to the store." We walk the road to the cemetery. It's about two or three miles long. It's the longest walk on earth. As we walk past people's houses, neighbors come out and stand by their gates paying respects to my mom. Mom loved stopping and greeting all these neighbors. Now they are saying goodbye to her for the last time. Funerals are definitely a whole community event. Everyone gathers, no invitations required. The band plays every 20 minutes and the pang of grief and pain pierces your heart every time the cymbals clash. Wailing begets more wailing.

We arrive at the cemetery. People gather by the coffin. Two pastors say sincere words from the Scripture and I hang on to every word because I believe every word and because it helps me cope with grief to place my hope

My brother and my dad are by mom's gravesite which is covered with wreaths before the head stone is placed. On the left is my sister's grave with an etched portrait of her.

in what it is unseen and not the dead body I see in front of me. Every word from Scripture uttered by the pastor is a breath of hope that fills my heart. Then a local government representative shares an equivalent of mom's obituary, speaking about mom's hard work for the trades cooperative. I like hearing how much mom was loved through the words uttered.

We say goodbye to mom at the grave site. There is no cement burial vault into which the coffin is lowered. The coffin goes straight into the damp, cold ground. We say goodbye again. Then we throw a handful of dirt onto the coffin and walk away in tears. The gravediggers make a mound of dirt over the coffin and now the grave site is marked. But there is no monument with mom's picture mounted yet because it takes about a year for the ground to settle. The wreaths are placed around the mound, forming a hill of dirt and flowers.

A big lavish dinner follows the funeral. That's another cultural practice I begin to question being enlightened by my American ideas. How can a retired former civil engineer with a pension of $100 per month afford to feed 150 people a meal that costs $400? In Ukraine, food is hospitality. People will judge you if you only serve fruit punch and ham and cheese sandwiches for guests to eat while they are talking. It has to be a sit-down dinner in a local restaurant with the appetizer, first and second course, drinks, and dessert.

I don't eat because I still can't process anything but grief. My mind is working hard on trying to wake up from this nightmare where my mom went to the hospital for an MRI on Monday and was dead on Wednesday after making a phone call telling dad, "I'm feeling better, Tolya." I picture my dad screaming all night long in agony from losing his life partner of 50 years (he reminds me that it was 50 years and nine months). I'm trying to shake off the nightmare, but it's not going away. I hear people eat and chatter nonstop. They show pictures to each other on their smartphones and I want to run away and go home. I look at my brother and see his red puffy eyes and I just want to go home with my dad and brother, but going home means facing the fact that when we return, my mom won't come out to the *podvirya* to greet us, kiss us on the cheeks three times, and tell us how happy she is that her kids are home and we are together again.

As I write this, the unfathomableness of it all hits me again. It hits me that I will never see my mom alive. But then Jesus reminds me that we do not grieve like those who have no hope. But we have hope. My mom's name is Nadiya which means hope. It is with this hope that I close this chapter.

Mom, age 18.

CHAPTER 18

"What Are You Up To Now?"

"Wow, You've Come a Long Way!"

I am on my way to do a keynote presentation on how language education contributes to inequitable opportunities for English language learners in K-12 schools in the U.S. I have come a long way, as one person keeps reminding me.

I am a long way from the potato fields and audiolingual method for learning English. I have come a long way from my first lesson of learning English when a teacher asked us, "So, who knows some English?" I raise my hand proudly and say eagerly, "I do. I can count to 10." I am 18 years old but I count like an excited kindergartener.

I have come a long way from seventh grade when I sneak into the school library to borrow an English-Russian dictionary even though German is the only foreign language offered by the school. I have come a long way since the days of third grade when my sister brought home German language home-work and I asked her to teach me how to say a book, a pen, a girl, and a boy. I use Cyrillic to write down German words: *дас бух* (das Buch), *штіфт* (der Stift), *медхен* (das Mädchen), *юнге* (der Junge). She explains to me what articles are in German, and that they are extra words to indicate if the word is feminine or masculine. I don't pay attention to the articles because they don't exist in Ukrainian, so I just write down the words without them. I have come a long way from knowing only one writing system: Cyrillic.

I have come a long way since the days of dreaming to speak in different languages as a young child to the days when I write my dissertation and give conference presentations at international linguistics conferences in my fourth language, which has now become my primary language and replaced the language of my childhood.

In my keynote, I share with my audience my own journey of learning languages. I tell my audience that learning a language is learning a culture and vice versa, learning a culture is learning a language. In these words, I relive my journey of learning language through culture and learning culture through language. I no longer subscribe to language as an inventory of structures that we teach our students without regard to context, the way I was taught. I tell my teachers that we don't need to continue teaching our students today the way we were taught years ago.

I try to inspire them with a new way of looking at language as a dynamic and living system for making meanings, as Michael Halliday conceived of back in the 1960s, calling the theory Systemic Functional Linguistics (SFL). I summarize his theory by saying that every time we speak, we do three things simultaneously: we represent ideas; we enact roles, identities, and challenge or maintain relationships; and we create discourse.

I pause to explain each and take more time to illustrate the second function language serves of enacting roles and identities. I bring the message of language as a system of choices in context, not only to my teacher audiences or for use in my research, but also use it in my own sense-making of how context determines our language choices. In particular, the interpersonal dimension of language is about how language construes our identity and positions us as people. This is of keen interest to me because of my never-ending negotiation of communication practices in which I find myself. I give an example of this to the attendees of my session.

"If I want to connect with the audience on a human level, I need to use a joke to kick things off with." I say, "It's good to be here in Georgia, where the climate and the people are very warm, unlike up North, where I'm from. I'm not saying the people are cold, but they aren't called the 'frozen chosen' for nothing. And the weather, yes, it gets very cold, but it keeps out the riff-raff." The teachers laugh and they see me as a human being, and not some distant talking head. The principle of how language as a system of choices in context is illustrated meaningfully when I describe the choices I make to construe myself as a relatable human being.

In my presentation, I continue to make jokes about the culture of small talk. I explain that weather is not just a neutral filler for small talk, but in the context of the current culture of global climate change, it is the topic under discussion, especially in the days of the polar vortex in January, and a temperature swing from a high of 73 degrees and sunny on Monday to 35 degrees and snowy on Wednesday in April. I use this theory to help me understand language and language users. This theory doesn't judge. It only describes. This theory of language helps me analyze language without judging it. It helps me understand the role of small talk, and the meaning of "Hi, how are you?" as a cultural practice because we need those cultural practices to build relationships. Since not all relationships need to be deep, we have small talk to stay shallow and to fill in the awkward silence of those long elevator rides and abrupt meetings on Monday mornings. I accept these cultural practices as my own now.

I conclude the talk with words to inspire teachers to help students view language as their resource to expand their identities and places where they belong. I realize I am also saying those words to myself.

I return to my office and discover the book *All Are Welcome* by Alexander Penfold:

We're part of a community.
Our strength is our diversity.
A shelter from adversity.
All are welcome here.

We will learn from each other.
Special talents we'll uncover.
There's a big world to discover.
All are welcome here.

You have a place here.
You have a space here.
You are welcome here.

I have a place here.
I have a space here.
I am welcome here.

I've written my way into belonging.

I open a children's book by Yuyi Morales where she says the things that immigrants struggle with become their sources of strength. I recall my language struggles, my cultural struggles, my identity negotiation struggles, and they are my strength. I am resilient. Without struggle, there is no growth. Learning new things requires courage. I am courageous.

Then I continue reading Yuyi Morales' words: "Someday we will become something we haven't even yet imagined. But right now, we are stories, we are resilience, we are hope. We are dreamers, *soñadores* of the world."

I am stories.
I am resilience.
I am hope.
I am a dreamer of the world.

Now I'm reading the Word of God, the words that are inspired and God-breathed.

> *"For you created my inmost being; you knit me together in my mother's womb." Psalm 139:13.*

*"**Before I formed you in the womb I knew you,** and before you were born I consecrated you; I appointed you a prophet to the nations."* Jeremiah 1:5

*"But **you are a chosen generation, a royal priesthood, a holy nation, His own special people,** that you may proclaim the praises of Him who called you out of darkness into His marvelous light." 1 Peter 2:9.*

*And, "I will be a Father to you, and **you will be my sons and daughters,** says the Lord Almighty." 2 Corinthians 6:18*

*"Fear not, for I have redeemed you; **I have called you by name, you are mine**." Isaiah 43:1*

*"I was **a stranger** and you invited me in." Matthew 25:35*

*"... **our citizenship is in heaven.**" Philippians 3:20*

I belong to the One who created my inmost being.

I belong to the One who knew me before He formed me.

I belong to the One who knit me in my mother's womb.

I belong to the One who knows my name.

I am a daughter of the Lord Almighty.

I am a chosen generation.

My citizenship is not on this earth. My citizenship is in heaven.

I have a new identity. This identity in Christ helps me reconcile all other identities. My identity is bound up in God's purpose for me. I am His.

*After this I looked, and behold, a great multitude that no one could number, from **every nation,** from all **tribes** and **peoples** and* *languages, standing before the throne and before the Lamb, clothed in white robes, with palm branches in their hands… Revelation 7:9*

I will forever belong.

Epilogue

The year is 2017. My boys are ages 11 and 15, and we are sitting in the dark in the Marcus Point movie theater watching *Wonder Woman*. Having boys who are being raised in America, I have been pleasantly introduced to the superheroes of the American pantheon. If you had asked me 10 years ago who Ironman was, I would have said it's my husband, because he does all the ironing.

Since then, I've been introduced to many other superheroes like Spider-, X-, Bat-, Iron-, and Super-man, but so far no wo-man. I'm thrilled to be introduced to the princess of the Amazons: Wonder Woman. As I watch this movie and follow her journey from the Isle of Themyscira to the no man's land of World War I, I begin to realize that she and I have a lot in common. She finds the new world she's been introduced to as being very foreign, with the clothing strange, the customs strange, and the food strange. In seeing her do this, I realize that she and I have followed the same path. She came from another country and another time, she was introduced to new clothing, new habits, a new way of talking. By the end of the film, she has adapted to her new homeland. She is part Amazon, part Western. She uses her well-honed Amazonian skills in the martial arts to help fight for democracy, a product of her own ancient Greece.

It's April 18, 2019. It's dinner time. We are having traditional American burgers. I ask my family, "What does it mean to be American? Is Mom American?" Nicky replies, "Mom, you don't want to lose that part of you that is also Ukrainian. You are Ukrainian-American." Rob replies, "America is an idea. It's freedom. It's struggle. It's resilience. It's hope." I am not just a Ukrainian in America. I am a proud Ukrainian-American who loves her freedom, who perseveres through struggle, and who continues to hope. Julian tells me, "Mom, you are you. That's all there is to it." I love the simplicity of those perspectives and yearn to simplify things without losing the meaning.

At its most general and basic level, memoirs are the written repositories of human memories. But not everyone writes to merely preserve memories. Some write to preserve their sanity, rediscover their identity, articulate their transformation, or become transformed in the process. For me, it is all of these things, but mainly to take time to engage through writing more deeply with my cross-cultural sense-making and understand myself and others better as well as be a window and a mirror for others. I hope this memoir gave you a glimpse of yourself, your culture, and a peek into mine. I apologize for the cultural generalizations.

Cross-cultural memoirs capture cross-cultural sense-making. They straddle both worlds, the new and the old, and in the in-between. The narrative of my cross-cultural sense-making is one reality, but recreating it for my vast audience is another. Whose story did I want to tell? The story my audience wanted to hear or the story I wanted others to hear?

When trying to appeal to my audience, I was feeling like I was losing something of myself. Maybe I put a positive spin on some things that didn't need it? Maybe I didn't depict Ukraine honestly enough? What if I was too critical? Was I critical enough? What if I wasn't honest with myself? One person helped me articulate this when she said, "When trying to reach our audiences, we lose ourselves." But as Rob always says, it doesn't have to be either/or. It can be both. You can tell your story and reach your audience with that story. I hope I've achieved both.

The biggest fear in writing this memoir was forgetting. Did I forget something significant? Did I remember enough? How do you tell your brain what to remember and how not to forget? Thus, memoirs are not about the number of pages or remembering all the events in the correct order. It's about remembering cross-culturally. I wanted to capture both above the surface and below the surface differences meaningfully, including the obvious ones that you can see with a naked eye, like green manicured lawns and sizes of homes, bathrooms, and walk-in closets as well as differences below the waterline, such as the construction of politeness.

In this memoir, I have crossed the terrains of culture, I have struggled with the conflicts of differences, and as a result, I have come to peace with myself, and my past, and turned my struggles into energy to move forward and to inspire others to do the same.

This journey allowed me to expand my worldview in ways that I couldn't have imagined. No simple potato field work would ever have been able to stretch my mind the way this experience has. My favorite saying about learning new things is, "A mind that is stretched by a new experience, can never go back to its old dimensions," by Oliver Wendell Holmes. I love all the stretching that I have experienced. My life is so much richer because of it and because of many of you who are here with me on these pages right now.

~ *Dr. Ruslana A. Westerlund*
   July, 2019

Timeline

My mom and dad on their wedding day. February 24, 1968.

FEBRUARY 24, 1968 – My mom and dad get married.

SEPTEMBER 6, 1968 – My sister Alla is born.

1969 – Dad builds the Buzhanka School.

FEBRUARY 16, 1973 – I am born.

SEPTEMBER 19, 1981 – My brother Bogdan is born.

APRIL 26, 1986 – Chernobyl blows its top. I am in 6th grade.

NOVEMBER 21, 1986 – Grandpa Fedir (my dad's dad) passes away (born in 1911).

DECEMBER 28, 1989 – grandpa Ivan dies. My parents accept Jesus and devote the rest of their lives to Christ.

MAY 1990 – I graduate from Buzhanka School of General Education (graduating class of 20 students)

JULY 1990 – I get accepted into Cherkassy Pedagogical University to study English.

FALL 1990 – Dad lays the foundation for the Buzhanka Baptist church.

AUGUST 24, 1991 – Ukraine becomes independent.

SPRING 1992 – John Guest, an American missionary visits Ukraine and delivers the Gospel to thousands of people at the Cherkassy soccer stadium. I accept Christ that day.

OCTOBER 10, 1993 – Dedication of the Buzhanka Baptist church.

SUMMER 1994 – a group of American missionaries comes to Lysanka. Caryl invites me (upon my mom's request) to come to Minnesota.

JUNE 1995 – I graduate with a degree (BA and MA combined) of teaching English.

MARCH 1995 – AUGUST 1995 – I work tirelessly on getting a travel passport, secure a visa, paying hundreds of dollars in bribes.

SEPTEMBER 3, 1995 – I emigrate.

SEPTEMBER 4, 1995 – I arrive in the United States.

OCTOBER 31, 1998 – Rob and I meet and fall in love.

AUGUST 15, 1998 – Rob and I get married.

FEBRUARY 16, 2000 – Alla dies from lung cancer.

DECEMBER 27, 2001 – Julian is born.

Rob and I on our wedding day, August 15, 1998.

2003 – Dad becomes a pastor of Vynograd church.

JUNE 27, 2005 – Nicky is born.

JULY, 2006 – I become a U.S. citizen.

MARCH 13, 2009 – My grandma Manya (baba Manya) passes away (born on March 15, 1925).

JUNE 20, 2018 – my mom dies from breast cancer.

JANUARY 14, 2019 – I begin writing my memoir.

About the Author

Photo by Paula White

Ruslana Anatolyevna (Deren) Westerlund was born in Ukraine in 1973. She is a daughter of Anatoliy Fedorovich and Nadiya Ivanivna Deren. She is a sister to Bogdan Anatoliyovich Deren, the most talented senior software developer in Amsterdam. She is a wife to Rob, who is the author of *First Person Omniscient* and the most balanced thinker in this polarized world. She is a mom to Julian, a lover of calculus and violin, and Nicky, a creative genius.

She has always been interested in cross-cultural thinking and sociolinguistics, which, along with academic training, allowed her to work as an interpreter, a guest speaker on cross-cultural communication, and a Ukrainian language teacher to many missionaries who took the Gospel to Ukraine from 1995-2005. *From Borsch to Burgers* is not her first book. She previously wrote a Ukrainian language and culture guide *Please, No More Food* (out of print). Ruslana is currently a researcher at WIDA at the University of Wisconsin-Madison, and a professor of linguistics at Bethel University. She loves gardening and lives near Madison, Wisconsin. To learn more, go to ruslanawesterlund.com.

Made in the USA
Monee, IL
22 April 2022

95236723R00142